Wolf Song

A Natural and Fabulous
History of Wolves

Catherine Feher-Elston
Illustrated by Lawrence Ormsby

JEREMY P. TARCHER/PENGUIN
a member of Penguin Group (USA) Inc.
New York

JEREMY P. TARCHER/PENGUIN
Published by the Penguin Group
Penguin Group (USA) Inc., 375 Hudson Street, New York, New York 10014, USA ·
Penguin Group (Canada), 10 Alcorn Avenue, Toronto, Ontario M4V 3B2, Canada (a division
of Pearson Penguin Canada Inc.) · Penguin Books Ltd, 80 Strand, London WC2R 0RL, England ·
Penguin Ireland, 25 St Stephen's Green, Dublin 2, Ireland (a division of Penguin
Books Ltd) Penguin Group (Australia), 250 Camberwell Road, Camberwell, Victoria 3124,
Australia (a division of Pearson Australia Group Pty Ltd) · Penguin Books India Pvt Ltd,
11 Community Centre, Panchsheel Park, New Delhi–110 017, India · Penguin Group (NZ),
Cnr Airborne and Rosedale Roads, Albany, Auckland 1310, New Zealand (a division of Pearson
New Zealand Ltd) · Penguin Books (South Africa) (Pty) Ltd, 24 Sturdee Avenue,
Rosebank, Johannesburg 2196, South Africa

Penguin Books Ltd, Registered Offices:
80 Strand, London WC2R 0RL, England

Most Tarcher/Penguin books are available at special quantity discounts for bulk purchase for
sales promotions, premiums, fund-raising, and educational needs. Special books or book
excerpts also can be created to fit specific needs. For details, write Penguin Group (USA) Inc.
Special Markets, 375 Hudson Street, New York, NY 10014.

Library of Congress Cataloging-in-Publication Data

Feher-Elston, Catherine, date.
Wolfsong : a natural and fabulous history of wolves / by Catherine Feher-Elston ;
illustrated by Lawrence Ormsby.
p. cm.
Includes bibliographical references.
ISBN 1-58542-358-0
1. Wolves—Folklore.   2. Indians of North America—Folklore.   3. Wolves—History.
I. Title.

GR730.W6F44   2004   2004058022
398'.3699773—dc22

Printed in the United States of America
1   3   5   7   9   10   8   6   4   2

This book is printed on acid-free paper. ♾

Book design by Carole Thickstun

For Mowgli,

beloved wolf,
and all our relations

"In the beginning of all things,

wisdom and knowledge were with the animals. . . . The One Above did not speak directly to man. He sent certain animals to tell men that he showed himself through the beasts and from them and from the stars and the sun and the moon should man learn."

Eagle Chief, *Wolf Pawnee*

Contents

Acknowledgments

*W*olfsong: *A Natural and Fabulous History of Wolves,* is the second in my *Naturesong* series, a collection of books about totemic animals and their relationships with humans. It is a companion book to *Ravensong: A Natural and Fabulous History of Ravens and Crows.* This seems appropriate, since ravens and wolves have an ancient and fascinating relationship.

It has been a decade since the initial concept of *Ravensong.* It was not my intention to allow a long lapse between *Naturesong* books, but in 1993, I decided to pursue doctoral studies and trundled off from northern Arizona for a long stay at the University of Texas at Austin. It was challenging to keep a home in Arizona, deal with Austin, write and work with wildlife and maintain any type of normal life. Graduate studies are not conducive to anything but graduate studies. I tried to do too much, and overextension led to a bad case of chronic fatigue syndrome—which knocked me out for two years.

During my recovery, I came to know a wolf named Mowgli. The first time I walked with the little red cub through the forests and wetlands of northern Arizona, he sniffed at the ground, detected mouse-scent, made a vertical leap and pounced down. Mowgli was a great jumper. The jump reminded me of the naming of Kipling's character, a child whose parents were killed in India's jungles by the tiger, Shere Khan. The orphan was found by wolves and adopted by the pack. Because he had no fur, he reminded the wolves of a frog and they named him "Mowgli," the little frog. Kipling's Mowgli was a boy raised by wolves. My Mowgli was a wolf raised by me. Working with Mowgli, I regained health and strength. Mowgli was beautiful, sensitive and intelligent. I had always respected wolves, but through my work with Mowgli and his family, I came to love them. Sadly, Mowgli was born with a birth defect that did not permit him to stay long on this earth. In my time with him and his family, I came to understand much more about wolves. I looked into global wolf status, wolf recovery in North America, aspects of wolf reintroduction in the Gila wilderness and the Rocky Mountains, the assault on wilderness in the Arctic and other wild places by various industries, and the amazing fact that wolves survive at all. After Mowgli's death, I was determined that his life will be remembered and his kind will survive.

Ravensong led me to Siberia and Central Asia and made me realize connections between certain cultures there and in North America. *Wolfsong* led me deeper into these regions and into connections between life and death, power and politics, light and darkness of the human soul, and the role of the wolf in these relationships. For many peoples, wolf is the teacher, the model for family life and the spirit of strength and endurance. Mowgli was a mentor to me, and I want to share wolf lessons with other people. Wolf survival is dependent on mutual understanding between people and wolves, and on overcoming human politics and emotionalism engendered by the ongoing debate about wolf recovery. Humans destroy what they fear and do not understand. This book is a plea for understanding and survival. I cannot expect everyone to love wolves and wilderness as I do, but I must try to help people understand the role of the wolf in the balance of things, and ask for acceptance of wolves in the world's few remaining wild places.

Wolfsong would not have been possible without the help and support of many people. I wish to thank my sister, Theresa Walsh of Wildcat Mountain, for grieving with me over the loss of Mowgli and helping me survive after the blow. Many thanks to my agent, Jenny Bent, and to my editor, Sara Carder, for her helpful remarks and patience. Thanks also to my illustrators, Lawrence Ormsby and his partner, Carole Thickstun. Thanks to Ed Bangs of the federal Northern Rocky Mountain Wolf Recovery Project. Thanks to the staff of Wolf Haven at Tenino, Washington. Thanks to the gentle wolves of Cocolalla, Idaho, and their Wolf People. Thanks to the Yellowstone wolves of the Lamar Valley, always willing and able to give tourists, scientists and rangers a thrill simply by existing. I thank the Mexican wolves of the Gila country and bless them. Despite federal recovery efforts, these little *lobos* face an uncertain future due to the greed and ignorance of a few cruel people in New Mexico and Arizona. Thanks to the tribal peoples and traditional voices that helped manifest this project. Thanks to all my relations, thanks to the Haudenosaunce, Dineh, Haida, Koryak, Skidi-Pawnee, Ojibway, Paiutes, Utes, to everyone. Thanks to my friends in Siberia. A special thanks to the Nez Perce for their love of wolves. To the Cheyenne people, who offered me a faculty position at Chief Dull Knife College, "Ha-ho." You have offered me new life and new hope, and a return to home in Montana. Walk in Beauty.

CATHERINE FEHER-ELSTON
Lame Deer, Montana
Summer Solstice 2004

Introduction

A longing cry echoes through the darkness. Plaintive, powerful, evocative of ancient mysteries, the wind carries wolfsong through the forest. The howl of the wolf is the call of the wilderness.

No creature provokes stronger human emotions than the wolf. For many, wolfsong evokes primeval memories and longing for times when Nature ruled supreme and the world was wild and free. To some, wolfsong evokes fear and loathing of the wild and untamed. Honored by tribal peoples as Father Wolf, protector of family and clan, revered by noble Romans as mother to the city's founders, Romulus and Remus, wolves also came to be feared and hated by medieval Europeans and their descendants. Wolf packs once flourished on five continents, but human persecution decimated wolf numbers. Why does the wolf stir such strong emotions and actions?

There was a time when Wolf and Man shared the earth and walked together in harmony. While echoes of the old times survive in our relationships with "Man's Best Friend," the dog, this time of harmony ended when people gave up the life of subsistence hunters and started farming and raising livestock. The first recorded bounties for dead wolves appeared in classical Athens. Shepherds in the hills of Attica were losing lambs to wolves, so the city established bounties for a short time. These shepherds developed special guard dogs to protect their flocks. Once the wolves understood the strength of the shepherd-canine alliance, their depredations on the sheep decreased. There was no longer a serious wolf problem, so the city rescinded the bounty. Descendants of these shepherd dogs still guard Greek flocks from wolves in northern Greece today.

While the ancient Athenians reached a balanced compromise with wolves, later Europeans did not. The transformation from wolf and human sharing the world to persecution and systematic annihilation of the wolf reached its full form in the Middle Ages. Respect for the spirits of Nature and animal emissaries of the gods turned to hatred with the ascent of Western Christianity. The wolf came to be regarded as the "Devil's Dog," and was feared, hated and hunted. The notorious tale of Little Red Riding Hood originated in the ignorance of the Dark Ages, and the brutal legacy of that story haunts wolves even today. Europeans exported their hatred of Wolf during their migrations and invasions of the New World.

When the Pilgrims arrived in Plymouth in the 1600s, they wrote of many wolves running through the forests. The indigenous peoples who helped the English survive their first years in Massachusetts did not fear wolves; they had always lived with them as part of their world. But European ignorance coupled with religious prejudice and fear of Satan's hounds prompted the English to set a penny bounty per murdered wolf. By 1640, the bounty had risen to forty shillings per wolf. To ensure the protection and sanctity of their City on the Hill and the advance of European civilization, wolves had to be exterminated. After a few years of European settlement, Virginia, Rhode Island, New York, Pennsylvania and New Jersey established wolf bounties. Shortly after the American War for Independence, the wolves of New England were wiped out.

As the Euro-Americans invaded the West, they sought to systematically exterminate wolves. An epidemic of wolf bounties spread throughout the North American continent from the early 1600s through the twentieth century. The Euro-Americans almost succeeded in exterminating wolves. Federal and state governments encouraged citizens to kill wolves. On the Great Plains, wolf killers received $1.25 per pelt. In Montana, from 1883 to 1913, the United States government paid bounties for 90,000 wolves. By the middle of the twentieth century, wolves were gone from most of the Lower Forty-Eight. Some wolves survived in Canada and Alaska. But by the end of the century, something strange happened: the hearts of the conquerors changed. Euro-Americans and other peoples reconsidered their persecution of Wolf. Many people now demand the restoration of Wolf to parts of his ancient domain. What caused this change of heart? The extinction of Wolf and Wilderness had been the quest of Euro-Americans since their arrival in the Western Hemisphere. What made their descendants demand reconsideration of and redress for past misdeeds? Was it the American romanticization of a world they had destroyed?

Was it a new understanding of ecology and the role every living thing plays in the dance of life? Was it guilt for the blood on the hands of the killers? Perhaps it was a reconsideration of the past, a recoiling from the horrors of human misdeeds, a realization of the power, beauty and necessity of wild survival that reflect sensitivities deep within the human psyche and a realization that we are linked to everything in the web of life.

Humans enter Wolf's domain in many ways. Deep within human consciousness lie memories of mythic times, when Man and Wolf shared the same prey and walked the world together. Wolf gave Man a most precious gift, cubs, which were raised with human children and became ancestors of modern dogs. From these times, when Wolf and Man danced with the spirits of Nature and learned from them, come myths. Sacred tales recited from generation to generation, myths reflect the oral histories and traditions of hundreds of thousands of generations. Myths were the foundations of human knowledge long before written words.

Relationships between humans, animals and spirits were interpreted through myth and the intermediaries between Spirit and Human, the shamans. The shaman was the precursor of the contemporary scientist, physician, pharmacist, psychiatrist, diagnostician, musician, artist and dancer. Chosen by the Supernatural as a conduit to humans, shamans learned from spirits how to cure disease; locate game; ensure fertility for human, animal and plant; bring rain and foretell patterns of the seasons. Certain spirits took a personal interest in the shaman and helped the magician fulfill community needs and obligations. The Wolf Spirit was a valuable guide for hunting peoples. For shamans, Wolf Spirit was a teacher and protector. Wolf Spirit demonstrated strength and courage in hunting, exhibited tenderness and love in the family circle and walked the pathways between the world of the Living and the Dead. Teachings from these ancient times persist in today's medicine people and the religious societies of many modern cultures.

Another avenue for learning about Wolf is modern science and ethology; animal behavior. While many scientists may not appreciate being compared to shamans and witch doctors, the fact remains that scientific inquiry supports behaviors explained in old myths and shamanic sagas. The division between the world of science and the world of Nature is artificial. It is a line drawn by arrogance, by people seeking to set themselves above their fellow creatures to justify exploitation of animal, mineral and other resources. Scientific inquiry and categorization provide tools necessary for learning, but not to the exclusion of integrated experiential knowledge and the ancient relationships between humans and other beings. Modern scientific tools play important roles in wolf reintroduction and survival, and they help people better understand the vital roles of wolves in ecological balance.

Wolfsong provides introductions to each of these avenues for understanding relationships between wolves and humans. The integration of myth, religion, ethology and science presents a more complete picture of history through wolf-and-human relationships. More and more people seek to

understand Nature and her ways. Wolf is one of her most effi-
cient and elegant creations. To understand Wolf, one must
enter a world of primeval beauty, a world where life and death
are inextricably linked. It is a world that has forever shaped
human belief and experience. Wolf's world is a land of shadow
and light, of love and terror, of forest, plain, desert and tundra.
A world of beauty and power, where family, pack and clan are
the primary focus of life; an ancient world of sacred bonds
between predator and prey. Wolf walks in legend between
myth and reality. The call of the wolf on a clear, cold night
is an invitation to enter this world.

Myth Time

Raven Creates Wolf

Pacific Northwest Athabascan

Long ago, at the beginning of all things, Raven, Creator of the World, was making new beings. He made the shining mountains rise from the sea and painted them their colors of green and blue and purple. He made the snow white. He created many beings, ancestors of life in the world today. Raven was a lover of life. He made the fleet-footed deer and the dappled caribou. He reached down with his mountain-maker's hands and made the fishes and gave them the sea for their home. He made the bears, the grizzlies and the polar bears, the brown bears and the black bears. He made the first human beings. He made the trees and painted each and every leaf on them. Raven made the birds and placed every feather in every pattern on them. He made the flowers of many colors. He made plants for medicine and food and taught the creatures the magical language for communicating with them. He brought all the beauty into this world.

One day, Raven decided to make a creature to be a teacher for human beings. He made this creature a furry, four-footed being, with intelligence, humor, strength, courage and compassion. He gave it a long snout, sharp teeth and long, strong legs for running great distances. He made the creature's ears beautiful, pointed and sensitive to even the faintest noises. The first one's color was dazzling white. Raven decided to teach it to fly. He put feathers on its front legs and taught it to flap them up and down, then he threw his creation high into the sky. The beautiful white one tried to imitate Raven. He flapped his front legs; the feathers moved, but they did not support him. He started falling back to the earth. He fell faster and faster. He fell so fast that the feathers were singed. His beautiful white coat turned to gray, with black tips from the burning. Raven realized it was better if his latest creation stayed on land and walked on four feet. But to this day, some of the descendants of this animal have fur with many colors on each hair, tipped with black at the very ends.

Raven made an entire family of these creatures, in many different colors. Their coats were gray, and black, and red, and brown, and white. Some had eyes of amber, some had eyes of brown, some had eyes of gray. Raven made the father and mother the rulers of the family. He made four children—two boys and two girls. He called them wolves.

"I cannot always be everywhere to teach others how to behave and how to hunt, so I want you to be models," Raven told the first wolves. "I have made you beautiful and intelligent. I have taught you to live as a family and be leaders and teachers for other creatures. Because you have a sense of humor like me, you may be tempted to tease and trick people and other animals. I know how that is. But if other beings ask you in the right way, with politeness and respect, you must help them, as I do."

Raven taught the wolves many things: how to hunt, how to make healing medicines, how to sing. He showed them delicious things to eat like blueberries and huckleberries and honey. He loved hearing the wolves sing at moonrise and sunrise.

Wolves love the moon and the sun. They are full of joy when they see them at the beginning and ending of every day, so they sing to thank the sun and the moon for sharing light and beauty.

Raven taught the wolves to pray for help when hunting, and how to call in game. He taught them the prayers for thanking animals willing to share life with them. He taught them to love and respect the game animals and all other life. He taught them to watch for other ravens and for crows, who would show the wolves the way to game so all could eat. Raven loved to play with the wolves, teasing them by grabbing their tails and stealing their food. Raven taught the crows and magpies how to tease the wolves, and the wolves learned the teasing game and played along—snapping their jaws at the birds when they came to share their meat and pretending to be annoyed.

The first wolf family was blessed and happy. Their children and grandchildren were born and roamed in lands all over the world. The descendants of these first wolves survive today, and they share the world with human beings and all other creatures. Wolf obeyed Raven's instructions and still serves as teacher to human beings. Today it is as it always was: wolves are willing to share life with human beings and others. As it goes with wolves, so it goes with the entire living world made by Raven.

The Wolf Star,
Wolf Medicine and the
First People

Great Plains Pawnee

Long, long ago, at the birth of all creation, all of the animals and spirits were invited to a Great Council. In those days, everyone—spirits, animals, plants and people—spoke the same language. Somehow, the brightest star in the southern sky, the red Wolf Star (Sirius) was left out. He did not get invited to the Council. His feelings were deeply hurt, so he watched from far away while all the other animals and spirits decided how to make the earth. Others made the world, and Wolf Star was not asked for advice.

Wolf Star blamed one called Storm Coming from the West for not inviting him to the council. Storm carried a bag filled with whirlwinds around with him. Inside this bag, he held the First People. Every evening when he stopped to rest, he opened this bag and let the people out.

"Come out now, it is time. Come on out," Storm said as he opened the pouch. Every night, the people would camp, hunt buffalo and feast, then sleep before returning to the bag with the coming of dawn.

Wolf Star sent one of his sons, a prairie wolf, to keep an eye on Storm and follow him around the earth. "Go down there and see what Storm is up to," he ordered.

Trailing Storm was hard work for the wolf, but he obeyed his father and followed Storm around. He eyed the bag Storm kept beside him. He was hungry from following Storm, and thought maybe there was something delicious inside that bag. "I wonder what is in that big bag," the wolf asked himself. "Well, I will just be patient and quiet. The right time will come and I will find out." The wolf followed Storm and waited for his opportunity to snatch the bag.

Storm grew tired and decided to take a nap. While Storm snoozed, the wolf ran up and took the whirlwind bag in his mouth and ran away with it. The wolf ran and ran. He ran far away from Storm. When he felt he had run far enough, he stopped and opened the bag.

All of the First People tumbled out. They were noisy and excited, looking forward to a big buffalo-steak dinner. They camped and got ready for the hunt. They looked for buffalo, but they could not find any. The wolf had carried them far away from the buffalo country. They looked around; they did not see Storm. They saw the wolf.

The First People were hungry. When they saw the empty bag and the wolf, they realized what had happened. They grew angry. They blamed the wolf. In their anger, they ran the wolf down. They killed him. It was the first time Death entered the world. It was the First People who brought Death into the world.

Storm Coming from the West awoke from his nap with a jolt. He had dreamed something terrible, and he felt fearful. He looked around for his whirlwind bag. It was gone. He searched the world. He found the First People. He saw what they had done. His heart was heavy, and he was very sad. He explained to the First People that they had done a terrible thing by killing the wolf. "You have brought Death into the world—now it will never leave. Now everything that is born will also die. That was not part of our plan, but now it is here. We cannot change it."

Storm Coming from the West told the people they would have to pray and make a medicine bundle. He told them to skin the wolf. He taught them songs to sing while they prepared the pelt and medicine bundle. He showed them what things to put in the bundle so they would always remember what had happened. Storm and the First People breathed on the bundle. Then, he told the people to pray and wait four days.

"From this day on, you will be called the *Skidi Pawnee,* the Wolf People," Storm told them. After four days, the wolf returned to life and went back to his father.

The Wolf Star watched everything from his home in the southern sky. To this day, the Pawnee call this star "Fools the Wolves," because it rises just before dawn and makes wolves think it is the opening of daybreak. The wolves call out to greet the new morning, but it is not really dawn. This is how the Wolf Star reminds people even today that when the Council met to make the earth, he was left out.

The Wolves and the Stags

Pacific Northwest/Tsimshian

One day, a long time ago, in the autumn of the year, when the leaves were turning yellow and orange and red and the streams were full of salmon, all of the wolves along the Nass River got together for a potlatch, a ceremonial giveaway of food and gifts. Entire packs came, with their leaders, their fathers and their mothers, their strong hunters and their young cubs. Even the lone wolves came, looking for mates.

Once everyone assembled, they sang long wolf songs. The howling chorus echoed from the river to the ocean and back to the mountains. All of the forest creatures heard the crying of the wolves, it was so loud. The howling forced the woodland creatures to flee—away from the whining. Even fishes in the streams buried themselves in sand or hid under rocks, it was so loud. The salmon's ears were especially sensitive to the din—they leaped over waterfalls and rapids to escape from the wolf songs. It is said that this is how salmon learned to jump over water cascades and overcome all obstacles in their travels from stream to sea and back again.

Finally, the howling became too much even for our Father Sun, and he set early that day and hid his head in the clouds to shut out the noise. The Moon, however, loved the wolf songs and climbed to the tops of the pine trees to hear the wolves singing. Her beautiful white face threw light onto the wolves and they were delighted to have such an elegant audience. They sang even louder to please their Moon sister.

After singing all day and half the night, their throats grew tired. So they started telling stories about wolf heroes and their deeds. Wolf warriors showed the cubs and young ones their battle scars. When not telling war and adventure stories, the wolves gossiped about this and that. They talked and visited all night. When the mist rose over the river and the dawn came, the tired little cubs fell into sleep.

A group of stags had gathered across the river, listening to the wolves' stories. Finally, one started laughing at the wolf adventures, and then the whole group guffawed. The wolves heard the deer laughter.

"Who dares to laugh at us, at the tales of brave wolves?" asked Gray Wolf, one of the oldest leaders.

No one answered; the stags just laughed harder and louder, snorting and snickering. Since the morning mist was heavy and thick, they felt safe, hidden from wolf eyes. So they laughed and laughed. Finally, Sun jumped back up into the sky and burned away the morning mist.

When the mist was gone, the wolves looked across the river. "Who is it that laughs at us, that finds our stories and our heroes so very funny?" the wolves asked. Then, they saw the stags and their beautiful pointed antlers. They saw the mouths of the stags as the deer laughed at them. They saw that

deer teeth were not sharp. The wolves were hungry for breakfast. Their mouths watered as they gazed across the river.

In an instant the hunters jumped into the river and swam
to the other side. The stags scattered as the wolves chased
them. To this day, wolves hunt deer. They know that they are
good to eat and have not forgiven them for laughing at their
heroes and their stories at that potlatch so long ago.

Trickster and the Wolves

Great Lakes Ojibway/Algonquin

*T*rickster's most beloved friend was a wolf. This is a story about that friendship.

One winter day, long, long ago, when the sky was clear and the ice froze hard on the rivers, Trickster was hungry, so he went out to hunt. He was walking across a frozen river when he saw some people far away, walking across the ice. Trickster was curious and he wanted to learn more about them. As he drew closer to them, he saw that they were not human beings, but wolves. Always the curious one, Trickster called to the pack.

"Oh, my nephews, what are you doing out here on the ice?" Trickster asked. Trickster was surprised to see them, but he tried not to show his surprise.

"We are hunting, Uncle," the wolves called back. Trickster, always eager to have others do work for him, saw an opportunity for free food. He knew traveling with wolves would assure him of tasty fresh meat. "Well, I am hunting, too. Let's hunt together," Trickster said. "I haven't seen you since you were babies, and you may not remember me. May I join your hunt?"

The wolves, preoccupied with the hunt, believed Trickster. "Well, you may join us, Uncle, but we don't think you will be able to keep up with us, since we have four feet and you have only two," the wolves replied.

There were five wolves in the hunting pack: an old one, who was the father of the group, and four young wolves. Trickster wasn't sure who was the head of the pack, so he stood, rubbing his eyes, pretending they hurt from the cold and he couldn't see well. "I can't tell who is the oldest and who is the youngest because my eyes are cold," Trickster said.

One of the young wolves introduced Trickster to the pack and bowed down before the oldest wolf and said, "This is our father." Trickster took a good long look at the wolves, so he could tell who was who. He called Father Wolf his brother. They talked for a long time, and then the wolves told Trickster it was time to get going.

The wolves started trotting, looking for game. Trickster tried to keep up, but he quickly tired. The old wolf saw Trickster's exhaustion. He felt sorry for Trickster. So he fell back and said, "You cannot keep up with us. But we can let the others go on ahead. You and I can keep a few steps behind. . . ."

Father Wolf was clever. He understood that Trickster wanted to be with the pack, because Trickster tried so hard to keep up. But he also knew that Trickster needed constant motivation. So he treated Trickster like a juvenile wolf who was just learning to hunt and travel with the pack. He always walked ahead of Trickster, so Trickster would not give up and get lost.

The young wolves were tracking a deer. Trickster and the old wolf saw their tracks in the snow. The tracks showed that the young wolves had spread out, running toward the deer and trying to encircle it. The old wolf asked Trickster, "Which of my sons do you think will catch the deer first?" Trickster replied, "The wolf that jumps the farthest will catch the deer first."

Father Wolf gently said, "No, the wolf that jumps the closest will catch the deer first." Trickster knew that Father Wolf was right. But he didn't want to admit it. So he argued with the old wolf as they followed the tracks. Father Wolf led the way, and Trickster followed behind, insisting that he was right and the old wolf was wrong. Father Wolf told Trickster to be quiet, or else his noisy arguments would frighten away all the game.

As the two walked along, they found a tree with blood on its trunk. Tracks showed that one of the wolves had bumped into the tree and bloodied his nose. A wolf tooth was embedded in the tree trunk. Father Wolf told Trickster to pull the arrow out of the tree trunk. Trickster looked at the trunk. He didn't see an arrow. He only saw a wolf tooth. Father Wolf again asked Trickster to pull the arrow out of the trunk. "Why should I pull out a nasty old dog tooth and carry it around?" Trickster asked Father Wolf.

"I keep telling you not to talk so much," Father Wolf said. The wolf trotted over to the tree and pulled out the tooth, and it was transformed into an arrow. Trickster felt embarrassed because he had been rude to Father Wolf, who had treated him with patience and kindness. "I will carry the arrow," Trickster said. Father Wolf handed the arrow to Trickster.

The two walked on and caught up with the pack. The four

wolves had killed a deer, and by the time Trickster and the old wolf arrived, nothing was left but bones. The four wolves were full of deer meat, sleepy and happy with big bellies. Father Wolf told Trickster to make a place for some meat. Father Wolf started clearing a space for his portion of the meat. Trickster didn't see any meat. He thought the four young wolves had eaten it all. But remembering his earlier rude behavior, he obeyed Father Wolf, and halfheartedly cleared some space for meat.

Father Wolf told his sons, "Give Trickster half of the meat." One by one, the four wolves came to the spot Trickster had cleared and vomited up venison. They did the same for Father Wolf. Then Trickster and Father Wolf ate deer dinner, the same way that wolves' young ones are fed.

After eating, Father Wolf told his sons to make a house. One of the wolf-sons walked in a circle, and magically a wigwam appeared. The pack slept warm and snug in the wigwam that night. They lived in the wigwam all winter long. The four young wolves went out and hunted when everyone was hungry. But Father Wolf and Trickster stayed in that wigwam all the time.

Trickster was happy living with the wolves. He didn't have to work at all to get his food. He and Father Wolf told stories through the winter days and nights, while the young wolves hunted and brought them food every day.

The wolves saved the bones of every kill. They saved the bones so they could make grease and tallow from them. The wolves rendered the bones into fat and made it into tallow in

a special way. Every wolf knew the magic formula for making
tallow, and everyone knew that no one was supposed to watch
while the tallow was made. Father Wolf told Trickster not to
watch when tallow was prepared. "Please do not look at the
wolf preparing the tallow and grease. You are one who doesn't
like to listen and obey. But there is a reason why I say not to
watch. If anyone watches or peeks at a wolf when he is making
tallow and grease, the bone will slip right out of his hands and
hit that person in the eye."

Father Wolf told everyone to lie down and cover their
heads with blankets while one of his sons made tallow and
grease. Everyone did, but of course, Trickster, being curious
and naughty, was determined to sneak a peek.

At first, Trickster obeyed. He heard the crunch of teeth
gnawing on bones. As it happened, Trickster's blanket had a
tiny hole in it. Trickster peeked through this tiny hole and saw
the wolf chewing bones, with grease running down his snout
and chin. Suddenly, a bone slipped out of the wolf's hands and
hit Trickster in the eye.

"Yow, yow, yow," Trickster wailed. As he stood up, the blanket fell off. He created such a commotion that everyone else
stood up and their blankets fell off, too. Trickster lied and said
that the wolf making tallow had deliberately hit him in the eye.

"He did it. He punched me," Trickster said, pointing at the
innocent wolf. Father Wolf rushed over. "You must have looked
at him, that's why the bone hit you in the eye," Father Wolf
said. "You better start listening when others tell you things for
your own protection."

"No, he came up and punched me," Trickster grumbled.

The wolf stopped making tallow and grease. He had made a fair amount before Trickster interrupted the process. No one resumed the work. The wolves stayed at the camp for a couple of months. They hunted and brought back fresh meat every day. When the grease ran out, Trickster announced that he would make the next batch. He persisted in his lie, insisting that the wolf making tallow had deliberately hit him.

The wolves were surprised that Trickster had learned the secret of tallow-making. They didn't believe him. "Go ahead, make some, then," they said.

"All of you must cover yourselves with blankets and not look," Trickster demanded. The wolves covered up their heads. Trickster started imitating the wolf that had made the tallow, the wolf the deceiver had accused of hitting him in the eye. Trickster made a little grease, but it didn't take long until he was tired of working. He walked over and hit the innocent wolf with a bone. The poor wolf yelped and made a lot of noise. "He was looking at me," Trickster insisted.

The wolves did not believe Trickster. Father Wolf thought and thought about the situation, and he became worried that someday Trickster might do something truly bad to his family. He made a decision. Father Wolf decided that it was best to separate Trickster from the pack.

"We must go on with our hunting," Father Wolf told Trickster. "You cannot keep up with us. But we do not want you to be lonely. So, you may keep company with your favorite nephew." One of the young wolves liked Trickster very much. He was happy to stay with Trickster. He took good care of him and brought him fresh meat every day. Trickster was kind to his wolf nephew. He never hurt him; he loved him. The two were happy living in the woods that winter. Trickster loved Wolf Nephew like a father loves his son.

Wolf Nephew hunted every day, while Trickster stayed warm and snug in the wigwam. Every morning, Wolf Nephew left the wigwam to hunt. Every evening, he returned with deer or rabbit or something equally delicious for Trickster.

In early spring, after the ice had broken on the rivers and lakes, the sun was deep beneath the western horizon. Darkness descended and Wolf Nephew was not home. Trickster had a bad feeling. Fear gripped his heart. Wolf Nephew was always home before dusk. Trickster knew that something was wrong. "Maybe that wolf got lost in the woods," Trickster thought.

Trickster went into the woods and found a dry, hollow stump. He hit the stump with a huge branch. "Boom, boom, boom," the hollow stump sang like a big drum. Trickster called into the darkness, "Nephew, Nephew, come home, come home." All that answered was the sad sigh of the wind. The wolf did not come home.

Trickster could not sleep that long, lonely night. The next morning, he left the wigwam before the first light of dawn, determined to find his nephew. He followed the wolf's tracks and walked a long, long way. He walked all day long. By late afternoon, he found a place where his nephew had chased a deer. Deer and wolf tracks led to a river. Deer tracks appeared on the far side of the river, but no wolf tracks.

"My nephew must have fallen in the water," Trickster said. "The water spirits, the *manidog*, must have grabbed my nephew and pulled him under. They must have drowned him."

A little crow told Trickster that the water spirits had pulled his nephew into the river when he jumped over the water chasing the deer. The bird told Trickster that the rulers of the manidog, the water-spirit chiefs, had ordered the killing of the wolf, because they knew that the wolf would always feed Trickster, and Trickster's insatiable appetite would destroy all of the game animals. Trickster started crying. He fell down on the riverbank and wailed. He didn't want to live anymore. Somehow, he found his way back home, back to the wigwam, where he had once been happy.

Trickster looked at his nephew's empty sleeping blanket. He saw his nephew's beads on the wall beside the bed. He held his nephew's beads and he kissed them. Trickster's grief turned to anger. "I will do the same to the manidog as they did to my beloved nephew. I will kill them," Trickster shouted.

Trickster put his nephew's beads in his medicine bag. He made war plans that night. He slept deeply, in part because of the exhaustion of grief, and in part because he was determined to be strong for his fight with the water spirits.

The next day, Trickster made his bow and arrows. He took a gigantic cedar log and split it in two for his massive bow. He split it twice to make it flexible. He made two huge arrows. Vengeance took his heart.

Trickster knew that the manidog would come up from the water on warm days to bask in the sun and sleep on the beach.

He went to the river crossing, where the water spirits had
drowned his nephew. Trickster climbed the hill overlooking
the bank. He turned himself into a burned-out tree stump. He
sang a medicine song; he called in warm weather for four days.
He called in hot days with no wind. So it was, hot and sunny,
for four days. Trickster waited patiently.

The manidog felt the warm weather and came up from the
water to bask in the sun and sleep on the warm, sandy beach.
Trickster stood watch on the hill, staring at the water. When
he saw a great swirling and twirling of the water, and the
movement of massive coils, he knew that the manidog had
come. The manidog look like huge snakes when they come
up from the water. Many came to bask in the sun and doze
on the sand. Two of the great chiefs of the manidog came as
well. These chiefs, called *ogima,* were the largest of the giant
serpents.

One giant snake spied the burned-out tree stump. He told
the others, "I never noticed that big old tree stump standing
on the hill before. I wonder if that is Trickster. He can take the
shape of anything."

Another snake said, "Oh, that can't be Trickster. He is not
a strong enough manidog to change like that. You worry too
much." The first giant snake said, "Well, I am going over there
to find out."

He slithered up the hill and coiled himself around the tree
stump that was Trickster. The snake squeezed the stump.
Trickster was strong, and he didn't feel anything. The second
time, the great snake squeezed a little bit harder. And again, a

third time, a bit harder, with all of his strength. By the fourth time, Trickster was hurting. He almost cried out, and was having trouble breathing, when the monster snake let go. "Oh, it's just an old stump. That isn't Trickster," he announced. He went down the hill to the beach for a sunbath.

As the sun climbed higher, the day grew hotter. Trickster watched and waited. The manidog grew sleepy. They slept deeply in the spring sunshine. When he was sure they were in deepest slumber, Trickster changed back into himself, took his bow and arrows into his hands and quietly climbed down the hill to the beach. He saw the high chiefs of the water spirits. He knew they were the ones who had ordered the killing of Wolf Nephew. Silently, he walked through mountains of monstrous snakes. He walked right up to the sleeping chiefs. He notched his arrow, drew back his bow and aimed. His arrow found its mark in the side of one of the sleeping Snake Chiefs. Then he turned, notched his second arrow and bent his bow. His second arrow hit the second chief. In an instant, all the manidog fled into the water. Trickster was left standing alone on the beach.

The manidog Snake Chiefs were wounded, but they were not dead. Trickster was determined to follow them to their home and kill them. He sat on the beach, thinking and plotting. A little bird flew down and sat on a branch, staring into the water. The little bird stared and started, leaning over the river. Trickster watched the bird and wondered what he was doing.

Trickster asked, "Why are you staring at the water?" The

bird kept watching the water and answered, "I'm hungry. The manidog killed a wolf and dragged him down to their village beneath the water. I'm waiting for that wolf's guts to come floating up so I can eat them."

The bird's answer enraged Trickster. He wanted to strangle the bird. "Oh. Well, while you wait, let me give you a small gift," Trickster said. He took out Wolf Nephew's beads and put them around the bird's neck. He grabbed the back of the bird's head and started squeezing the beads. Just as he started, the bird slipped out of his hands and flew to a tree. The back of his head was spiky and fluffy where Trickster had grabbed his feathers. The beads fit snugly around his neck. "You *Mujiyunim,* rascal, good-for-nothing. You and your descendants will wear those beads forever. You will be called *gistumanisi,* kingfisher. And you will always wear my mark and the mark of my beloved nephew."

So it is that to this day, the kingfisher has a bushy head and a necklace of white. Trickster, a partner to the Creator, did make the world and had power. But he did not have the power to bring his beloved wolf back to the living world.

Trickster walked through the forest. He followed tracks and signs through the woods to the village of the Snake Chiefs. After a long time, he saw someone walking. He walked up to the person. It was an old woman. She was carrying a huge load of wood on her back. When she saw Trickster, she looked frightened. "Who are you?" she asked. "You aren't that wicked Trickster, are you?"

Trickster realized that the old woman was almost blind. He

answered, "*Noko* (Grandmother), if I was Trickster, I would kill you. What are you doing with all that wood?"

The old woman believed Trickster. "Well, we will use this wood to find Trickster. We will spread it all over and wherever it moves, he will be there. When we find him, the water spirits will send a great flood to drown him. Trickster attacked our chiefs with his arrows and almost killed them. I used all my prayers and medicine to save them."

When Trickster realized he was speaking with the medicine woman helping to heal the two manidog chiefs who ordered the killing of his beloved Wolf Nephew, he became angry. He decided to kill the old shaman, because she had healed the killers of his nephew. He asked, "Noko, do you sing when you doctor the chiefs?"

"Yes, the medicine songs help the healing," the crone answered. "Oh, what do you sing?" Trickster asked. "What do you call that song?"

"The name of the song is 'Trickster.' Here is the song:

Trickster, ho, notch of the arrow
Trickster, ho, notch of the arrow
I suck the point out with my mouth
I suck the point out with my mouth

As I sing this magic song, I give the chiefs special herbs and plants to make them strong again. They get stronger every day," she explained.

Trickster spoke with the old crone a long time and learned

all about her medicine ways. He thanked her for teaching him
the song. Then he asked her which way she was going. She
nodded her head toward the village. "Thank you, Noko,"
Trickster said. "You probably should be on your way."

As the old woman turned to go, Trickster hit her on the
head and killed her. He decided to disguise himself as the old
medicine crone. He took her skin and put it over him, he put
on her clothes and shouldered her burden of wood.

After a short walk, he arrived at the village. He did not
know which house was the house of the Snake Chiefs. He did
not know which house was the home of the old medicine
woman. As he stood on the edge of the village with the bun-
dled wood, a group of children ran up to him. "Grandmother,
Grandmother, welcome home," they cried. "You must be very
tired after your long day. We will help you carry the wood
home." They took the wood and helped Trickster to the old
woman's house.

Trickster rested in the old woman's house. It wasn't long
before someone came and asked him to doctor the Snake
Chiefs. "They are really getting bad. They need your medicine," the messenger explained.

Trickster went to the chiefs' house. As he entered, he saw
a wolf skin hanging in the doorway. It was his nephew's skin.
Anger rose in Trickster's mouth; his heart burned for revenge.
But he hid his anger. Several snakes kept staring at Trickster
in the house. They stared and said to themselves, "That sure
doesn't look much like the old medicine woman." Trickster
heard the snakes' thoughts and felt the snakes' stares. He spoke

to them in the old woman's voice, "I can't do much for these chiefs if you keep staring so hard at me." The snakes looked away. Trickster turned to the chiefs, shook a gourd rattle and started singing the medicine song:

> Trickster, ho, notch of the arrow
> Trickster, ho, notch of the arrow
> I suck the point out with my mouth
> I suck the point out with my mouth

As Trickster kneeled over the first Snake Chief, he saw his arrowhead protruding from the giant snake's body. He leaned over and pretended to be sucking the arrowhead out. He moved the arrowhead around, and pushed it deeper into the snake's body, pushed it deep into the snake's heart and killed him. After he killed the first Snake Chief, he turned to the second monstrous serpent and did the same thing. Then he stood up and threw off the old woman's skin and ran out of the house. He ran across many piles of wood. The villagers saw the wood move, they recognized Trickster and yelled out, "There he is, there he is!"

Trickster ran and ran. He laughed with the success of his revenge. The manidog chiefs were dead. Trickster had avenged his nephew's murder.

But the surviving water spirits were angry. They sent a great flood. They tried to destroy Trickster. But Trickster fled to a giant pine tree and climbed it. He survived the flood and was glad he had avenged the loss of his nephew. But revenge did not bring Wolf Nephew back. Trickster's tears mixed with the flood.

Nothing would ever bring back his lost one. Trickster loved that wolf more than anyone or anything. Trickster cries for his lost wolf even to this day. On cold, clear nights, he cries to the wind, and other wolves hear his sorrow and his pain and answer back.

Wakayabide and the Wolf

Great Lakes Ojibway/Algonquin

*O*nce, long ago, when human beings and animals spoke the
same language and both human and animal honored the
spirits and walked with them every day, there lived a man
called Wakayabide. That name, Wakayabide, means, "You can
see his teeth plain." Wakayabide had no lips, so everyone
could see his teeth. He had no skin over his stomach, so you
could see his insides, too.

Wakayabide had a wife. He went hunting every day. He
took his bows and arrows, and he tracked game and brought
meat home every day. It was strange. Wakayabide brought
home meat every day—but he never brought the entire body.
He brought back part of a deer, or part of a moose, but never
the whole thing. He never brought home a heart or a liver. His
wife wanted heart and liver. Every day she asked him to bring
her heart and liver. She wanted to make her blood strong. Finally, Wakayabide said, "All right, I will bring you deer heart
and liver tomorrow."

Wakayabide was in a difficult situation. He did not kill the
deer himself. The wolves made the kills, and they ate the liver
and heart. Wakayabide would cut the rest of the meat and

bring it home. He never told his wife or anyone else how he hunted.

He would awaken before dawn and leave the wigwam every morning. He knew the wolves killed the deer for their breakfast. Wakayabide could run fast. He could chase a deer until the deer was tired. Wakayabide waited in the woods. Before long, a deer ran by, chased by a wolf. Wakayabide joined the hunt. He chased the deer. Neither deer nor wolf paid attention to Wakayabide.

It was a long chase. Wakayabide ran fast. He lost a moccasin. Still he ran. He lost his second moccasin. He kept running. He ran and ran. He lost his leggings. He lost his apron. Still he followed the deer and the wolf. Twilight fell and evening came. Wakayabide kept up the chase. As twilight skies turned indigo, the wolf leaped on the deer. He brought down the deer and grabbed the heart and liver. Wakayabide had promised that liver and heart to his wife. Wakayabide followed the wolf. He was desperate to get the heart and liver for his wife.

Twilight turned into indigo and indigo turned into darkness. The night was cold. Wakayabide had lost everything but his buckskin belt, which held his hunting knife. Wakayabide had nothing with which to start a fire. "I shall die now, for the sake of my wife, who wanted that meat," Wakayabide told himself. "I shall prepare a place to die."

The wind moaned through the trees and the pines whispered as Wakayabide looked for a place to prepare for death. He found a big, hollow pine log. It was dry in there and sheltered from the wind. "This will do," Wakayabide said. "I will lie down inside this log and sleep until Death comes for me."

Wakayabide stretched out inside the log. The wind blew harder, making a cold night frigid. Wakayabide dozed, but he could not sleep. It was too cold for sleep. Wakayabide tossed and turned and drew leaves around him, trying to get warm.

After several uncomfortable hours, he heard footsteps. The footsteps were coming toward him. "Death has come at last," Wakayabide said. Wakayabide closed his eyes and waited.

"Wakayabide, why did you follow me?" a strong voice asked. Wakayabide opened his eyes and looked into the darkness. Standing before him was a huge wolf. "It was a foolish thing, you following me. You know you will never catch up with me when I run. My grandson, why did you run so hard? Why did you chase me? I have come back to help you. You will freeze to death tonight if I do not help you. I want to give you my strength. I want to protect you, my grandson. I am going to teach you things. I will tell you what to do. But tonight, you will sleep warm."

The wolf told Wakayabide that the next morning he must arise and head south. "You will find some people camping south of here. Make friends with those people. There will be an old woman who will get timber for a big night fire. You will have a nice spot by that fire to warm yourself. But tonight, you will sleep deep inside my fur."

The wolf shook himself and produced a warm, wolf-wool blanket. "Take this, my grandchild," the wolf said. He shook himself again and produced another blanket. "Here's another one. Take it to stay warm," he said.

The wolf shook himself four times and made four magic wolf-wool blankets. Each time he did this, he became smaller.

Finally, the giant wolf was a tiny version of himself and lay down beside Wakayabide. "Now we will both sleep warm," said the wolf. "Sleep well, my grandchild."

The next morning, Wakayabide awoke, warm and refreshed. The wolf announced, "Now, I will take back my blankets, and I will show you some of my power." The miniature wolf shook himself four times and became his true, gigantic self once again.

"I am your protector. Anything you ask me, I will give you, if it is in my power. Now watch me again," the wolf explained. He shook himself four times and became small, as small as a little finger. "Wakayabide, now listen to me. Put me inside your belt; keep me beside you always. I will be with you and help you for the rest of your life. If you have trouble and need help, call me. I will always help you."

Wakayabide followed the wolf's instructions. He sewed the now-tiny wolf into his belt. He ran south, as the wolf had told him to do. Wakayabide ran until he found a big fire. The fire was outside a large village of many wigwams. One of the houses was really long—it was a *midewigwam,* a medicine lodge, where sacred dances and ceremonies were held.

An old lady left this medicine lodge and came to the fire. She was surprised to find Wakayabide there. She could see the inside of his stomach. She saw his teeth. His appearance frightened her, and she ran back into the medicine lodge. She told her husband, "I am afraid. I saw a *manido* (spirit) beside the fire. I could see his guts and his teeth, and he is naked."

The old woman's husband was the village chief. He called

his people together and told them, "There's a stranger by the fire. He is our guest."

The chief's son, always a mischievous teaser, smiled and wryly said, "Well, it can't be one of our in-laws, can it?"

The older people took the chief's son aside and told him, "You can't act like that. You can't speak like that. A manido has come to us, so we'd better be good to him. If you are mean and disrespectful, he could come and kill you or do harm to the village. We'd better be good to him."

But the chief's son persisted in his teasing, and some of his friends supported him and insisted that the stranger couldn't be a true manido. "Why, you can see his guts. He's no manido," they said.

The chief insisted that his people treat the visitor with respect. "Be good to that stranger. Be kind to him."

The chief's son was called Madjikiwis. He announced, "I am going to see my new in-law," and walked out of the wigwam. As he left, he lifted his club. It was a huge club with a big ball at the end of it for hitting things. When he picked it up, sparks flew around the room and thunder and lightning filled the sky. He had great power.

He went to Wakayabide. "My friend," he said. "I offer you a new home. A home with us, here, in this village. I want you to marry my youngest sister. When you enter the wigwam with me, you will see three young women—my sisters. The tallest one will invite you to sit with her. Politely say 'No thanks.' The medium-sized one will invite you to sit with her. Just say 'Thanks, but I have a place.' Then walk right up and sit beside the smallest one—she will be your wife."

Wakayabide and the chief's son entered the medicine lodge. The tallest sister invited Wakayabide to sit beside her. "Come, sit right here. Sit right here with me," she invited. "No thanks," said Wakayabide.

Then the medium-sized sister asked Wakayabide to sit beside her. But Wakayabide said he had another place to sit, and he walked right up to the youngest sister.

The smallest sister smiled at him but said nothing. Wakayabide sat right down beside her. Wakayabide and the youngest sister were happy together.

Wakayabide looked around the medicine lodge and saw the splendor and power of his new brother-in-law's club and the wealth of the family. His wife told him, "There are many things you should know about us, and about this place. I will teach you. We have all kinds of games here. But I want you to be careful. The people here are dangerous. They kill each other in these games. Do not enter any of these games, for you will not last long if you do. Be careful."

The entire village heard that Madjikiwis had a new brother-in-law. Powerful men had courted the sisters. News of the youngest one's marriage swept the village. Everyone was curious about the new husband. Everyone crowded into the lodge. Everyone wanted to meet him.

The first man entered the lodge and said, "I've come to see my brother." He was a giant, tall, strong man. There was a big boulder in the medicine lodge. This giant man came and sat on the rock. He carried a big tobacco pouch. He told Wakayabide, "I'm glad you are here. I am glad to see you. We have so much fun here. We play many games.

We would like you to join us. We would like you to play with us."

Wakayabide smiled, but remained silent. The giant man announced, "Now, I will show you my power." He picked up the boulder and tossed it from one hand to the other, as if it were a child's toy ball. He walked toward Wakayabide, and deliberately stumbled, acting as if he would drop the boulder on the bridegroom. But he didn't drop the rock. He smiled and put it down.

"You see that power. That is the kind of man I would be if I had married that woman," the suitor explained. "But now she is yours." The big man offered Wakayabide tobacco from his tobacco pouch. Wakayabide filled his pipe with tobacco and smoked with the man.

Wakayabide knew that this big man was taunting him. He knew the suitor was trying to frighten him away from his new wife and new home. Wakayabide had his own power. He decided to use it to teach the arrogant suitor a lesson. He decided to shoot him with his arrow, not to really hurt or kill him, just to graze him. Wakayabide drew back his bow and his arrow barely grazed the man in his thigh. The man grabbed his tobacco and ran outside.

Everyone in the village heard the man's roaring laughter. "Aha-aha-ha-ha-ha. I give up. Finally, I find a man better than I am. Here is a manido. I give up. I won't bother him anymore. He is a manido."

Another man came to see Wakayabide the next day. The first man was really a grizzly bear disguised as a big man. The second man was really a polar bear. Wakayabide realized that this was quite an unusual village, where people changed into

animals and animals changed into people. The new man announced, "I've come to see my brother." He brought out his
tobacco pouch and a long pipe. He sat on the big boulder. He
smoked with Wakayabide. Then he said, "Now, I will show
you my power."

The man stood up and leaned over the rock. He held out
his big hands and scratched the rock with his long, sharp nails.
Sparks flew everywhere around the rock and the lodge. Flames
blazed on the rock. "You see that power," the suitor said.
"That's the kind of power I would have if I had married that
woman."

Then, he sat down and refilled his pipe with tobacco.
Wakayabide knew he was being tested. He took out his bow
and drew it back. He grazed the second suitor on the side of
the head with the arrow.

The second man ran outside, laughing. "Aho, you are a
better man than I," he yelled. "My brother, I give up. I won't
bother you anymore."

A third suitor arrived the next day. This one was truly human. He was strong and muscular. Wakayabide's wife warned
him once more about the peculiar ways of her village. "These
men are testing your power. You be careful. Tell no one of your
true power or strength, and don't play any games with these
men," she insisted.

As the man raised the blanket and entered the lodge, a tor-
rent of water entered with him. It was water with a strong current, the waves were frothy and red—it was red-clay water. The
flood filled the lodge. Wakayabide was being swept away. His

wife grabbed him and tied him with her belt, and held him close to her. The water rose and rose. It covered Wakayabide's head. He could not breathe. Just as his lungs were about to collapse and he was about to drown, the flood receded. The water disappeared and the lodge was completely dry.

The red-clay water man pulled out his tobacco pouch and pipe and sat on the giant rock and smoked. "You see, that's what kind of man I would be if I married that woman," he said.

Wakayabide took out his bows and arrows once again. This time, he aimed at the giant rock in the middle of the medicine house. As he pulled back the bow, he prayed to the arrow and asked the arrow to hit the rock and break off a piece of it and make that piece hit the red-clay water man.

The rock sliver hit the man's arm and scraped it. "Oho, I cannot win with this man. He is too good for me. I give up!" he exclaimed as he left the medicine lodge.

Three powerful suitors had challenged Wakayabide and tried to drive him away. They could not do it. Wakayabide's power was too strong.

Early the next morning, the village crier walked through the streets, inviting everyone to a lacrosse game. "Today we have a lacrosse game. Everyone should come. Madjikiwis's brother-in-law must play, too."

Wakayabide's wife was worried. She took him aside and told him, "I don't want you to go. Please don't go—they will kill you."

Wakayabide put his arms around his new wife. "They can't kill me. At least, I will go and watch. Even if I don't play, I can

watch the game." Wakayabide left his wife's house. He carried
his bow and arrows, but he forgot his belt—the belt with his
wolf guardian inside.

Wakayabide went to the lacrosse game. His brother-in-law,
Madjikiwis, was losing the game. Madjikiwis gambled his
moccasins, his fine beaded belt, his fine knife, his buckskin
breeches, his shirt and his beautiful silver necklace on the
game. He lost everything. He saw Wakayabide watching
the game. He hoped his in-law would come and help him.
Wakayabide heard his new brother's thoughts. He leaned on
his bow as he watched the game.

One of the suitors, the grizzly bear, came to Wakayabide
and handed him a lacrosse stick. "Here, brother, come and
play," he said.

Wakayabide remembered his wife's warning. "I don't know
how to play," he lied. "I cannot play."

"You must play," the grizzly bear insisted. "I can teach
you—take the stick." It didn't take much coaxing. Wakayabide
wanted to help his in-laws. He wanted to play that game.

"Well, all right. I will try," Wakayabide told the bear. He
took the lacrosse stick and entered the field.

The ball came toward Wakayabide. His bear partner said,
"Take the ball and run for the goal."

Wakayabide grabbed the ball with his stick and headed for
the goal. The bear followed him—but jumped on his back and
split his skin to the bone. Wakayabide dropped dead right
there. The people gathered around and cut him into pieces.
Everyone in the game took a piece of Wakayabide and cooked
it for dinner.

When Wakayabide did not come home that night, his wife was worried. She asked about him. No one would tell her what had happened. The wife refused her dinner. She could not sleep. The wolf knew something was wrong. He started howling and the howl came outside the belt.

The worried wife heard the howl. She looked around. It sounded like a wolf calling far off in the woods. She listened. She realized it was coming from inside the belt. She took the belt and found a little pocket inside. She opened the pocket and found a tiny wolf inside. She put the little wolf on the floor. She knew this had something to do with her husband's medicine power.

The little wolf shook himself four times, and with each shake, he grew bigger. Finally, he was his immense self. He thanked the woman, then dashed out of the medicine lodge. He ran all over the village. He gathered all the bones of Wakayabide. He put the bones together in the shape of a man. One bone was missing—the elbow. The wolf searched all over the village for that elbow. He could not find it.

The wolf trotted to a hill overlooking the village. He saw smoke rising over some trees. He realized there was a house out there. He ran to the little house. He sat outside the doorway and peered in. He saw that a young woman was living in that house. She was gnawing on Wakayabide's elbow bone. The wolf sat down and stared at the woman.

"Mmmm—this is just so delicious," she cried when she saw the wolf. "I suppose you want this bone when I am done. Well, it is just so delicious, I just don't know when I will finish."

The wolf moved nearer to the woman. He waited, but he

grew impatient. The woman taunted the wolf. "I just may keep this bone forever," she said.

The wolf lost his patience. He jumped at the woman and grabbed the elbow bone. He raced back to the skeleton and carefully placed it in its proper position.

The wolf sang a magic song. Then he shouted, and the bones came together. He shouted again, and flesh covered the bones. He shouted again, and Wakayabide's eyes opened. When the wolf shouted a fourth time, he leaned over and breathed into Wakayabide's mouth. Wakayabide was alive again.

"Grandchild, you did not listen to me," the wolf guardian said. "See what happens when you don't listen? I came to save you. Now get up, and let's go home."

They walked together to the medicine lodge. The worried wife was happy to see them. "I found that wolf in your belt. You better always keep him with you from now on," she said. The wolf made himself small once again and went inside the belt.

The next morning, everyone acted as if nothing strange had happened. The village crier announced another lacrosse game. "It is time to play another game," the crier called. "Madjikiwis's brother-in-law should join us again."

Wakayabide grabbed his bow and arrows and started out the door. "My husband, do not go," the wife cried. "They will kill you again."

Wakayabide consoled his wife. "I want to go," he said. "I want to teach that fellow who jumped on me and killed me a lesson." This time, the wolf was beside his grandson. This time, Wakayabide remembered to wear his belt.

Wakayabide joined the lacrosse game. He saw the grizzly bear and called to him. "Brother, come here—I want to play with you," he yelled.

"Oh, fine. Here I am," the bear answered, and joined Wakayabide. The ball came toward them. "I will show you how to play," the bear announced as he grabbed the ball. Wakayabide, with two arrows in his hands, followed the bear.

Wakayabide buried the arrows in the bear's back. One of them pierced the bear's heart and killed him. Wakayabide walked away. The people came and cut up the bear and cooked him for dinner. In that strange village, this is how they got their food. They played games and killed each other and ate each other.

The next day, the man-bear came alive again. He had a lot of power. This was a strange and magical place.

The Wolf Husband

Olympic Peninsula/Quinault

A long time ago, a young girl from a village near the snowy mountains went out to collect wood for the family fire. This girl was kindhearted and gentle, and her gentleness was reflected in her beautiful face. While she was in the woods, a wolf cub saw her. He thought she was the most beautiful being he had ever seen. He followed her all that day. He followed her to the edge of the village. He waited for her all the night. The next morning, when the girl went into the forest to get wood, the wolf cub followed her again. Every day for four days, the cub followed the girl and waited for her at the edge of the village every night.

On the fourth day, the cub decided to meet the girl. He followed her. When she stopped to drink from a spring, he sat at the base of a huge cedar tree and whined. He made himself sound lost and pathetic. The girl looked around. "Oh, a lost puppy. There is a lost puppy out here," she thought. "I will find it and take it home."

The girl found the cub. At first, she did not realize that he was a wolf cub. She took him in her arms and hugged him. "Are you lost?" she asked. "Are you hungry?"

She reached into her burden basket and pulled out some

dried venison and gave it to him. That evening, when the girl returned home, she had plenty of wood and a strong, handsome cub with her.

Her family saw the joy in her eyes when she looked at the cub, and welcomed him into their house. As was the custom among the Quinault, the cub slept at the foot of the girl's bed. Time passed and the two grew up together.

The girl grew straight and strong, and she became a young woman. Her skin was healthy and radiant, her hair glossy and dark as a raven's wing. Her inner beauty shone through, and she was one of the loveliest maidens in the village. The cub grew strong and handsome. His eyes were like golden amber; his coat was a mix of red, blond and brown, a cinnamon color: a red wolf. His majestic head and beautiful open face, with a cream-colored mask, revealed sensitivity and intelligence. The two shared a secret.

The wolf and the young woman loved each other, and when they were fully grown, the wolf showed her that he could change into human form. Every night, the wolf changed form and became a handsome man. They slept together in the same bed; they were husband and wife. In the false dawn, before it was light, he would return to his lupine shape.

In time, as is the way of life, the young woman became pregnant. When her parents noticed her body changing, full of life, they demanded to know the name of the father. The girl would not tell them the name of her husband and lover. Finally, when the time came, she gave birth to five beautiful, plump wolf cubs, four males and a female. This was a high-

caste family, and they were ashamed when they learned about
the wolf father. They called the village together and her father
killed the wolf. They tore down their houses, put out all the
fires in the village and moved away from the place. They took
their canoes and sailed away, leaving their poor daughter and
her children alone to die.

So, the poor young mother was abandoned by her own
people. She cried for her wolf husband. She cried for her lost
human family. She sat in the ashes of her house and waited for
death. Crow saw all of this with her shiny eyes. She saw no
shame in the love between the wolf and the girl. But she saw
great shame in the behavior of the human beings.

Crow took pity on the girl. She took some fire coals and
placed them between two clamshells and placed them close to
the empty village. Then she went to her favorite perch, a giant
hemlock tree on the edge of the village, right next to the ruins
of the girl's house. From this place, Crow watched everything
that happened in the village.

"Young woman, young woman," Crow called out to the girl.
"Look up here, in the hemlock tree, I am here. Look at me."

The girl looked up. Her eyes were red from weeping. She
was pale, and she had lost weight from so much grief. "Yes,
what is it, Crow? How can I help you?" the girl asked.

"Oh, my dear child, it is I who will help you," Crow said.
"I know you need fire to cook and stay warm. Sit quietly for a
while after I fly away, and listen. You will hear a crackling
sound. Follow that sound and you will find a gift from me to
you—you will find a fire," compassionate Crow explained.

The girl sat still for a long time. She listened and heard a crackling. Following Crow's instructions, she followed the sound and found the fire Crow had made.

Even with Crow's fire, life was hard for the young mother. Since her father had murdered her wolf husband, she had to care for the five wolf children alone. The only way she could survive and care for them was to dig for clams and other shellfish and gather seaweed on the beach. Through the love and care of their mother, the cubs grew quickly. After a time, the mother noticed that every time she left her camp to collect food, she heard the sounds of singing and dancing. On four separate days, she heard the sounds. When she heard the singing and dancing on the fifth day, she threw down her clam digger and walked back to the camp.

She did not take the direct path to the camp, but cut through the undergrowth. She crept up to her house and peeked through a crack to see what was happening. She saw four handsome boys dancing, and a beautiful little girl keeping watch toward the beach—where their mother was supposed to be digging clams.

The surprised mother took a deep breath and then walked into the house. "Why didn't you tell me you could take human forms? Why didn't you show those forms to my parents, to my village? If everyone had seen your human form, your father would be alive and no shame would have come upon me and my family!" the widow cried out. Then, she collapsed in tears.

Her children sat down. They were ashamed of the pain they had caused their mother. They remained in human form after this. As the children grew, their mother made little bows and arrows for the boys, and she taught them how to hunt small game and birds. She taught the girl how to collect shellfish, and how to make seaweed soup, and the sacred names of plants and herbs and how to talk to plants in a magical language to heal sickness. When the boys grew bigger, she made them big bows and arrows and taught them how to shoot deer and elk. She taught them prayers for calling in game, she taught them prayers of thanks after an animal has offered itself and she taught them prayers for purification after a kill.

She made them swim and bathe in the sea every day so that they would grow strong enough to hunt whales. The mother made harpoons and lines of cedar and sinew, with sealskin floats. The family built a hunting canoe. When everything was ready, the boys went out to the sea, praying for whales. They were blessed with the hunt and brought back so many that the whole beach smelled like whales.

Crow had nestlings of her own by this time. She watched the beach and the ruined village from her nest, high on cliffs overlooking the bay. The island where the village people had moved was just across that bay. One day, she saw a big fire in the village. She flew down to see what was happening with her favorite friends. As she flew over the beach, she saw the whales. She flew into the village and the children, who were grown up by now, offered her rich whale meat. They gave her all she could eat, and told her to come back any time if she needed more. Crow filled herself up, and stuffed her gullet with whale meat for her own nestlings.

When Crow started for her home, the young mother asked her not to tell anyone that she and her children were alive and well. "Please, Crow, when you return, cry loudly and wail, and act as if you are in mourning, so no one will come and hurt us," the worried mother begged.

Crow's eyes lit up. "Oh, I love secrets," she said. She flew back to her nest. But while Crow loves to learn secrets, she can never keep them. As she flew over the new village, she called out, "Caw-caw-caw. You should see what is on the beach near your old homes. So much whale meat, the wolf boys are great whale hunters."

Some of the people heard Crow, but everyone knew what a gossip she was, so no one really believed her story. But when Crow gave some of the whale meat to her young ones, one of them gobbled it so quickly that she choked, and a piece of whale meat shot straight out of the nest and onto the ground outside a house in the new village. Some people saw it, and recognized whale meat. Only then did they believe what Crow had told them.

The people talked it over. They decided that they should go back to their old village. They loaded up their canoes and went back. They apologized to the young widow and admitted that they were wrong to have judged her and treated her so cruelly. They gave her many gifts and held ceremonies to honor the spirit of her wolf husband. The wolf sons became great chiefs and brought great honor to their mother and always made sure that there was plenty of meat for their mother's people. It is said that the Wolf Clan came from the love of the wolf husband for the young woman.

Sea Wolves

Haida/Haida Gwaii (Queen Charlotte Islands)

A long time ago, a man was walking along the beach some-where on Haida Gwaii, the lands of the Raven People on what Europeans call the Queen Charlotte Islands, off the coast of northern British Columbia. He found two wolf cubs on the beach; he worried that they had lost their mother and father, so he took them home and raised them.

One day, after the cubs were grown up, he watched them swim out into the sea and kill a whale. They brought the whale to shore, to share the meat with the man. Every day, it went like this. Every morning, the wolves hunted in the sea and brought back whales. They brought back more than they and their human father could eat. Pretty soon, there was so much whale meat on the beach, it started going bad. It started stinking. When Great Person Above saw the waste of the meat, he made a great storm and brought down a fog so the wolves would not find any whales to kill.

The wolves went out hunting in the ocean. The waves grew higher and higher, and the fog grew thicker and thicker. They could not find their way back to their Man-Father. They had to stay out there, in the ocean. They transformed into orcas, sea wolves. Their black-and-white bodies and their distinctive masked faces show the original wolf markings. Because of the love of their Man-Father for them, and his care, they hunt whales and many creatures in the sea, but they will never harm a human being.

The Wolf Daughter

Koryak/Kamchatka, Siberia

long time ago, in a village called Kichiga, there was an old woman called Kytna. She lived with her husband and her daughter. A large wolf family lived near the village. One day, the daughter, called Ralinavut, went out walking. She did not return home that evening, or the next. Her parents were worried. They went to their neighbors in the village and asked, "Have you seen our beautiful daughter Ralinavut?"

The villagers asked one another if they had seen the girl. Her parents and friends went to settlements nearby and asked if anyone had seen a young girl, with hazel eyes and jet-black hair. "Have you seen her, have you seen our Ralinavut?" they asked.

They looked for her everywhere. No one had seen her. Her parents and her village were sad. They feared that she had lost her way in the snow, and had frozen. The same day that Ralinavut was lost, the wolf pack moved away from the region. No one guessed that the wolves had made her part of their family and taken her away as one of them.

Her mother Kytna did not feel in her heart that her daughter was dead. She kept waiting for her return. She waited patiently. She looked for her every day. Three years passed. But the lost daughter did not come home.

Kytna was beloved by the spirits. She was a shaman. She picked up her drum. She prayed, she played and sang all night. She asked her spirit helpers for assistance.

The next morning, she told her husband, "Our daughter is alive. She lives with wolves, far away in the north. She is near a place called Talkap. Do you remember three years ago, the big wolf pack near our village? There were twenty-eight wolves in that pack. They enchanted our daughter and took her away. They took her far to the north. I will go and bring our daughter home."

"Old woman, that is very far away," the husband said. "It is so far, it is so cold. You will get lost on the tundra."

"No, old man, I will not get lost," the shaman mother replied. "I know how to get there."

"Well, then we must prepare things for your journey," the old man said. He prepared food packs and warm clothes for his wife.

With the first rays of dawn, Kytna turned her face north and started walking. She prayed to her spirits. She turned into a wolf. With their big feet and long legs, wolves travel quickly on the snow.

By evening, Kytna found a reindeer-herders' camp. She changed from a wolf back to her human form and walked up to the camp.

"Welcome, old woman," one of the reindeer-herders said. "Have you walked a long way? Where are you from and where are you going? Why are you walking? Come and sit with us. Come and eat."

Kytna accepted the hospitality. "Thanks for your offer. I am going north to Talkap," she explained.

"Talkap, that's a long, long way. It is a long and difficult way if you walk," the herder responded. "Walking could be dangerous. We have good reindeer and we can give you a reindeer and sled. You will travel fast that way. You are welcome to have a reindeer."

"Thanks for your kindness," the shaman said. "But I feel more comfortable traveling by foot. I will walk north."

"Well, you know best," the reindeer-herder said. "But we have good reindeer and you are welcome to them."

Kytna resumed her northward trek with the dawning of the new day. As soon as she had walked a hundred steps, she transformed into a wolf. The wolf trotted steadily north. The friendly reindeer-herder watched her go. "Aha, so that is why she refused our reindeer gift," he said.

By midday, Kytna met a wolf. She stopped to talk with him. "Oh, brother, please tell me," the wolf shaman asked, "have you met any unusual wolves in a pack to the north? The kind of wolf who is both wolf and human?"

"Good day, sister," the polite wolf replied. "Maybe I can help you. Far away, in the north, beyond Talkap, there is a big pack, twenty-nine wolves. I was once their guest; I did notice one unusual wolf. It is my thought that she was not a real wolf. She seemed more like a human. Her form was wolf, but she had hazel eyes."

"Oh, likely, that was Ralinavut, my daughter," Kytna said. "I am looking for her. She has been away from home for three years."

"You call her Ralinavut?" asked the wolf. "I have heard that name. In that pack up north, there was a female wolf with that name. Good hunting, sister." The wolf nodded and trotted away.

Kytna ran north. She came to a camp of Chukchi reindeer-herders. She changed into human form and entered the camp. "Welcome, welcome," the Chukchi said. The Chukchi were lonesome for company and happy to have a guest. "Welcome, here is reindeer, here is fat. Come, sit down and eat."

Kytna sat down and rested on a bed of soft reindeer pelts. She ate her fill of reindeer. After she finished her meal, the herders inquired, "Who are you and where do you come from and where are you going? An old woman, alone, on foot, where are you going and how can we help you?"

Kytna appreciated the kindness of the Chukchi and their hospitality. "I come from the south, from far south from a place called Kichiga," she said.

"That is a long way from here. You are a long way from home. Kichiga—I was there once," one of the Chukchi herders commented.

"Tell me, please," Kytna asked, "are there many wolves around here? Is there a large pack around here and do they bother your herds?"

"Oh, yes, we have a big wolf pack around here, twenty-nine wolves," the friendly herder replied. "We are sick and tired of them. They take our reindeer from time to time. It's a good thing we have our strong and vigilant dogs, our malamutes, to help us. They let us know when the wolves are around. But the wolves still take our reindeer from time to time."

Kytna leaned forward and told the Chukchi, "Those wolves took my daughter away from home. Now she lives with them, with their pack, as part of their family. She has been gone for three years. I don't know if I will be able to bring her back home. We miss her."

"We will help you in any way we can," the Chukchi said. "But now it is time to sleep. You need rest. You have walked a long way."

"I must get up early," Kytna said.

The camp awoke before dawn. They offered Kytna tea and food. They offered her reindeer and malamutes to help her find her daughter. "Thanks for your kindness," Kytna said. "But I better travel alone."

Kytna travelled north. She travelled to a place where wolves were eating reindeer they had taken and killed in the night. This was reindeer from the Chukchi herd. Kytna saw the pack and became a wolf. She circled around the feasting pack. Kytna started chanting:

Many wolves here eat their food . . .
Among them must be Ralinavut.

She sang in wolfsong, as she circled the pack.

The wolf daughter, Ralinavut, felt something. She shivered

and stopped eating. "Someone is here," she thought. "Who is looking for me here on the tundra?"

The shaman mother drew closer. Circling one more time, she sang:

> These wolves are thieves.
> Here lives my daughter Ralinavut.

The wolf daughter realized who had come. "It is my mother looking for me," she thought. "Who else could it be? It is my own mother." She moved toward the voice and quietly sang back in wolfsong:

> Momma, how did you come to find me?
> Momma, I wish you had not come.
> I have been a wolf so long now
> Taken in by wolves
> In the family of wolves.

The shaman mother drew closer to her daughter and made a third circle. She sang her answer:

> Ralinavut, daughter of hazel eyes, you are a human being.
> Like us, you have a human name.
> Ralinavut, awaken. Ralinavut, wake up.

Ralinavut could not help herself. She ran to her mother. "Momma, momma, why are you here? How did you find me?" Kytna answered her daughter, "My heart was ice. Life was

cold without you. I've come for you and I will not leave without you. I am your mother. Let us run away from the wolves
when they are not looking. There is a Chukchi reindeer village
close by. We can rest there. I am very tired, my daughter. I
came all the way up here on foot."

Ralinavut's heart melted at her mother's voice. "All right,
we shall go," the wolf daughter replied. They ran to the village,
returned to human forms and entered the reindeer camp.

The Chukchi greeted their return with astonishment and
joy. "Oh, what a brave old woman, what a brave mother," said
the Chukchi herdsman. "Not only has she returned from the
wolf pack, but she has taken her daughter back from the
wolves. How brave she is, what a woman."

Kytna and Ralinavut rested. The Chukchi gave them food.
They rested and then Kytna announced, "It is time to go home."

"Your home in Kichiga is far away," the Chukchi said. "Let
me take you to your home on my reindeer."

"Oh, you are kind," Kytna said. "But we don't need your
reindeer. We will go on foot. We will leave early in the morning."

The next dawn, Kytna and her daughter left the Chukchi.
The people watched them leave. After the two women walked
a hundred steps, they were gone and in their places were two
running wolves. They were running very fast. "Aha, so that is
why they refused our reindeer," the Chukchi said. "Wolves
will get there much faster."

Kytna and her daughter ran back to Kichiga. The old man,
Kytna's husband, looked out from his house. He saw two
wolves running toward the village. They ran side by side.
"That must be my Kytna and our daughter coming home to

me. That must be my wife and my girl coming home." He ran outside, toward the wolves.

The village was in pandemonium. People did not know what to think, they did not know what to do. Two big wolves were running toward their homes. "Wolves are coming. Wolves are coming," they yelled.

The old father told them to settle down. "They are not wolves," he said. "They are human beings. Why would wolves run straight into a village in the middle of the day?" Suddenly, there were no wolves. Kytna and her daughter were walking in the snow. They came home. Kytna brought her daughter home.

Artemis and Apollo Lycius, Deities of Light and Wolves

Classical Greeks

From the days of the Mycenaeans through classical Greece and to this day, the twins Artemis and Apollo have been associated with light, medicine and prophecy. While Artemis is still remembered as the Virgin Huntress and protectress of women in childbirth, often portrayed with her quiver of arrows, her bow, the crescent moon and a wolf, people seem to have forgotten Apollo's ancient association with wolves. Apollo is remembered as Apollo Helios, a sun god; as the champion of reason and embodiment of all that was good about Greek civilization. Few remember that one of the oldest names for the twin children of Olympian Zeus and a woman, Leto, is Artemis and Apollo Lycius, "Artemis and Apollo of the Wolves."

Leto was the daughter of the Titan gods Phoebe and Coeus. Her name means, "the bright, hidden one." Zeus, King of the Gods, fell in love with her. It is said that after Leto conceived her twins with Zeus, the high lord of Olympus, jealous Hera, wife of Zeus and Queen of Heaven, was determined to destroy Leto and her unborn children.

Hera decreed that no place in Greece should accept Leto. She chased the poor expectant mother from Crete to Samothrace, from Troy to the Cyclades. In her attempts to escape Hera's wrath, Leto assumed many forms and disguises.

As the time came for the birth, Leto changed into a wolf and swam ashore on an island that sailors called Ortygia. Ortygia was once a nymph named Asteria, who refused the amorous advances of Zeus, out of respect for Hera. Spurning his advances, the nymph flung herself into the sea. Zeus punished her by turning her into a barren island that floated on top of the sea, never anchored in one place. As soon as the wolf-formed Leto swam ashore on Ortygia, four columns rose from the seabed and held the island fast. This arid, deserted island's destiny was to be the birthplace of two of the most important Olympian gods, Artemis and Apollo.

Hera prevented her daughter Eileithyia, protectress of childbirth, from helping to relieve Leto of her twins. Leto suffered birth pangs for nine days and nine nights. The ancient goddesses Rhea, Amphitrite, Dione and Themis travelled to Ortygia to help Leto. They tricked Hera and enabled Eileithyia to relieve Leto. With the coming of dawn, the young gods were born. Artemis was first born, and then Apollo. As soon as the children emerged, swans flew across the sky; sea nymphs and neriadae sang songs of joy. The island was flooded with sunlight and gold and was renamed Delos, "a place visible and known to all." Since that time, Delos has been the center and focal point of the islands called the Cyclades, "circle," which wind around the first and most celebrated sanctuary of Artemis and Apollo, the twins of light and reason.

Leto had changed into a wolf, and other wolves came to help her. They swam onto the island at sunrise, as the twins were being born. Artemis and Apollo were worshipped as *Lycius,* "of the wolves." Wolves sing at first light, the time of the twins' birth. The Greek word for dusk, *lykofos,* means "wolf-light." The word for daybreak is *lykavyes,* "wolf dawn."

Apollo is the male embodiment of light, power and knowledge. Artemis, his sister, is the female embodiment of these qualities. Apollo's symbols are the sun, the bow and the arrow. Artemis's symbols are the moon, the bow and the arrow. Gods of enlightenment and healing, they could also bring quick and painless death through their "darts."

The power of light overcomes the power of darkness, and Apollo and Artemis make plain to humankind things that are hidden. Because of her mother's pain and suffering for nine days, Artemis always comes to the aid of women in childbirth, when she is invited.

Followers of Artemis and Apollo honored wolves. The coins of Argos, a city protected by Apollo, bore the likeness of a wolf through the fifth century B.C. The Greeks cast a bronze sculpture of a wolf who protected Apollo's sanctuary at Delphi. The wolf caught and killed a robber in the temple of Pythian Apollo and also guided pilgrims to the city along the Sacred Way. At the south end of the Athenian Acropolis lie the ruins of an old temple to the divine twins; it is called the *Lykeion,* "the wolf house." Aristotle taught at this temple while he was writing his *Inquiry into Animals.*

The relationship between Artemis, Apollo, wolves, light

and prophecy is so ancient that no one really knows how far back it goes, or when it started. Likely, it evokes memories of the primeval Indo-European past, when ancestors of both the Mycenaeans and Dorians lived as hunters, somewhere near the Caucasus Mountains, and hunted with wolves as their companions. The wolf is sacred to these ancient twin gods of prophecy, and they serve as intermediaries between the living and the dead and among the past, present and future.

Who Speaks for Our Brother, Wolf?

Seneca/Haudenosaunee

A long time ago, our people were many, and our families kept growing. The land could no longer grow corn or beans or squash. The water became dirty. The animals of the forest moved away from our houses and fields. The land and the forest could not support everyone. A council was held. Many great leaders and their clans attended. Representatives from the human and animal tribes came. The Six Nations of the Iroquois, the Haudenosaunee, "People Who Live in the Long Wooden Houses," sent their representatives. He Who Understood the Language of Water was there. She Who Understood the Longhouse, keeper of Haudenosaunee knowledge, was there. He Who Understood the Storms of Winter attended. Wolf, Brother of Wolf, was there. It was decided that runners would be sent out in all directions to find land with plenty of room, and water, and food for everyone.

After many weeks, all the runners returned. Each had found a land with plenty. But Wolf, Brother of Wolf, had not yet returned. The people waited for four days, but still Wolf did not return. The elders decided to convene the land council, anticipating that Wolf would join them soon. The elders listened to the reports of every runner. All the land sounded good. After listening, they discussed which way to go, to bring the people to a land where they could settle and stay forever. After four days, they agreed on lands to the west. Then, a villager called out, "But wait, where is Wolf, Brother of Wolf? How can a decision be made until we hear from him? Who, then, speaks for Wolf?"

No one answered. People looked at one another and then stared at their feet. They knew they should wait for Wolf's return. But things were getting crowded, and everyone was anxious to move on. It was decided that they would move to the new lands in the west. People began the move west. Finally, at last, Wolf, Brother of Wolf returned. He asked about the new lands and was told their location. "But you have chosen the center home for many wolves, for a big community of wolves," he responded with alarm. No one wanted to hear what he had to say. People moved onto the new lands and thought it was a good decision.

After some time, food started mysteriously disappearing, and people saw wolves moving in the shadows beyond their villages. At first, the people did not mind wolves taking some of their food. They said, "Well, it is fair. We share some food with the wolves in return for a good place to live—that seems a fair exchange."

As the villages grew bigger, wolves became bolder. They started coming into the villages looking for food. At first they came at night. But after a while, they came in daylight and darkness, seeking food. Their boldness made the people nervous. They decided that they should make a plan to drive off wolves, should they come too near the village. The people became dissatisfied with this scheme, because it demanded constant vigilance and time devoted to watching out for wolves, rather than preparing fields and crops, building houses and getting ready for the coming winter. The elders held a council. Everyone agreed that neither providing wolves with food nor driving wolves off was good. They realized that it was hard for wolves and people to live closely together. They realized that they had made a mistake by moving into lands that belonged to so many wolves. They realized that they should have listened to Wolf, Brother of Wolf.

Some villagers said they should hunt down the Wolf People and destroy them. But the elders said that this was not a good choice, for then they would be wolf-killers. They did not want to be a murderous people. It was better to take life only to live and share land with the wolves and other creatures. The elders said that perhaps the people should consider a move farther away from the center of the wolf lands.

A council convened. Wolf, Brother of Wolf, was consulted along with all the other elders and clan representatives. The people decided to move away from the center of the wolf community. To this day, the councils of the Haudenosaunee include representatives to speak for the Wolf People.

Many generations later, new people came to our lands in wooden ships. They have a different way of living. What we do with much discussion, much thought and consideration, they do with tools and eating the earth. They plan for winters, but not for many tomorrows and the Seventh Generation. We have not been able to teach them to ask this question, "Tell me, brothers and sisters, tell me, who speaks for our brother, Wolf?"

Shamanic
Echoes

Power of the Wolf

*N*ature is the mother of life, the prime mover of the universe. Before humans and their gods, Nature existed. She is the cosmos, the beginning and end of everything. Humans understood this from the dawn of their existence. Our ancestors were hunters, dependent on the cycles of the seasons, the bounty of plants for food and medicine, the patterns of rainfall and the fertility of animals. They learned about the world and how to survive in it through careful observation and sharing of knowledge from generation to generation. Most of human experience is founded on ancient hunting days and ways. In those days, humans lived together in families and clans, like the wolves, ravens and game animals who were their teachers. They shared the same hunting grounds; they studied animals and learned from them. Humans treated other creatures with respect and acknowledged the unique ties that bind all life together. There was no division between the mundane and the mystic. People understood that every creature had a spirit; every rock, every tree, every plant and herb and spring was a living entity.

Evidence of human understanding of the power of Nature

is manifested in paintings, frescoes and petroglyphs dating back 16,000 years, in caves and tombs from the Siberian *taiga* to France, Italy, Spain and North Africa. The people who created these works were conduits between Nature and human, shamans.

Shamans were the first intermediaries between the world of humans and the forces of Nature. A shaman was an individual chosen by the powers of Heaven, Earth and the Underworld, by the realm of the seen and unseen, to act as mediator between worlds.

In hunting societies, through the power of the spirits, the shaman located herds to feed and clothe the people. Through prayers and dance, shamans ensured fertility and the continued survival of human and animal; ensured that there would be clean water and abundant plants. It was the shaman, through prayer, dance and trance, who called upon the spirits to drive out disease and illness from the community. Through communication with the divine, shamans learned the sacred nature and language of plants and how to approach them and use them for healing. The shaman was an essential figure in society—sacred, respected and sometimes feared.

To be chosen by the spirits as a shaman was a serious responsibility and obligation. Once the spirits chose, the initiate could not escape. Stories were told about people chosen by spirits to do the arduous and dangerous work of a shaman, and the consequences if one tried to avoid one's sacred duty. The shaman underwent two stages of initiation. In the first, initiation by the divine spirits, the shaman, through visions, dreams, trances and other ecstatic means, was taken by the powers and killed by them. The chosen one was torn apart, piece by piece, and devoured by the powers of Heaven, Earth, Fire, Water and all other forces. After death, the spirits rebuilt the shaman and restored the human to life. In the second step of shamanic learning, the shaman learned traditional prayers, names of spirits, mythologies, sacred languages of plants and animals, herbal and pharmaceutical knowledge and techniques for reaching the world of the Dead.

In the shamanic ethos, there were three planes of existence. These were: World Above, or Heaven; Middle World, the earth we walk upon; and the Underworld, the world beneath. Shamanic societies believed that these three worlds were linked together by a Tree of Life, and that shamans could travel up and down this tree, between worlds. Shamans travelled through prayers, music, trance and hallucinogenic plants. Instruments like the shaman's drum and the stringed oud were magical devices that enabled the shaman to "ride" across and between worlds. Various spirits—animal, plant, mystical guides, gods and goddesses—assisted the shaman on these journeys.

Shamans had spirit helpers, many of whom were animal spirits. It is easy to understand why, in archaic hunting societies, the Wolf Spirit would be a most powerful ally for a shaman.

Wolf is strong and hunts by day or by night. Wolf is a connection between worlds—the World of the Living and the World of the Dead. Wolf is clever, loyal and slow to anger—and it is important for shamans to have reliable allies. Wolf persists in hunting and ensures that food is shared among the entire pack. Often, Wolf Spirit travels with Raven Spirit on their supernatural hunts. To have such allies would clearly be beneficial to a holy person in a hunting society.

The old hunters believed that prayers to game animals enticed the animals to offer their meat for the good of the human tribe. The concept of animals sacrificing themselves for humans when addressed with respect through proper prayers was common among shamanic peoples. Among most of the world's surviving subsistence-hunting societies, hunters pray and "call in" the deer or other game animals. Offerings are made to the animals and spirits. Among the tribes of the American Great Plains, tobacco, sage and cedar are offered. Among peoples of the Southwest, corn pollen, corn meal, tobacco and sage may be offered. All these peoples offer prayers of thanks and ask forgiveness for any pain inflicted by the hunter. Success in the hunt indicates acceptance of the prayers and blessings from the animal spirits.

Wolves and ravens are universally regarded as creatures of prophecy and as mystical intermediaries between the World of the Living and the World of the Dead. Both are affiliated with magic, medicine, healing and transformation. In Nature, the two are often seen together. In many societies, from Siberia to Canada and the Pacific Northwest, Raven is regarded as Creator of the World; in ancient Celtic society, Raven was one of the forms of the Great Mother Goddess, and when she travelled her consort, Cernunnos, the Stag-God, and wolves often accompanied her. Raven is universally identified with hunting and is recognized in many societies as a Keeper of Game. Many hunters pray to Raven for success. The Athabascan ancestors of today's Dineh honored both Raven and Wolf. Raven was honored as Black God, the God of Game Animals. Ancient hunting rituals connect the Dineh of the high mesas and deserts of the Southwest to the heart of the Siberian taiga.

In the old hunting way of the Dineh, shamans and hunters prayed, fasted and entered a sweat lodge before hunting, to be transformed from human beings into hunting animals—wolves, to communicate with Black God, the Master of Animals, and then went forth as killer-hunters, to bring back food for the People. Sacrifices were made to Black God and the Animal People; hunters spoke a sacred hunting language after the transformation and during the hunt. After the hunt, they returned to the sweat lodge to be purified from the bloodshed and to resume their human identities. The introduction of livestock to the Dineh pushed the old hunting religion into the cultural background, but to this day, the Dineh honor Black God and remember days when men changed into wolves to hunt and bring food to their people.

Shamanic echoes ring through mythology. In myth, as in Nature, wolves and ravens are connected. Odin, ruler of the old Norse Gods, was accompanied by two ravens, Hugin (Thought) and Munin (Memory); and two wolves, Freki (Hungry One) and Geri (Greedy One). It is said that after Odin and his brothers made the world, Odin travelled the earth. He was lonely, so he made the First Wolves, Freki and Geri. He needed companionship and help with hunting. Freki and Geri were his constant companions; wherever Odin went, his wolves were beside him.

Odin loved the beauty and affection of his wolves. With

his wolves beside him, he was no longer lonely. All of the world's wolves are the children of Odin's wolves.

Odin also made the First Ravens, Hugin and Munin. Odin had only one eye, so he needed them to keep an eye on the world. Every dawn, he sent his ravens out, one to the east and one to the west, to fly around the world and bring back news of the day. Every evening, they returned to him, perched on his shoulders and told them everything they had seen.

Odin's wolves helped Hugin and Munin. The ravens were excellent locators of game, and they were always hungry. But they were not strong enough to kill game animals by them-selves, so they scouted for Freki and Geri. The wolves would make the kill and share the meat with the ravens. It is still so today: ravens and wolves travel together. Many hunting peoples maintain that the raven finds the game and leads the wolf to it, and that together they share food and survive.

Odin found happiness watching wolves and ravens play together, and he loved the joy both ravens and wolves found in the world. When Odin made First Man and First Woman, Embla and Ask, the parents of all humankind, he told them to learn from the wolf. He explained that the wolf would teach them how to hunt, how to raise a family and how to protect each other. Following instructions from the Viking King of Gods, the wolves shared their world and their wisdom with the early people. In the Viking world, to be a Wolf Brother— a member of the Wolf Clan, *Ulfhedna*—was a great honor. Brave Viking warriors turned into magnificent wolves after they died, and they ran with Odin and his wolves.

In old Norse legends and sagas, Odin is said to have had children who were both wolf and human. They were called Vosung (Wolf Young) and Wulfsung (Wolfsong). They were fabled warriors who assumed wolf shapes in battle and when hunting.

It is said that on the Day of Destiny, *Ragnarok,* when the Aesir, the Noise Gods, die, a giant wolf named Fenris will devour Odin. Fenris is the son of Loki, the Viking Trickster God. Fenris was born a trusting and gentle giant, but the Aesir feared him, because they knew he would ultimately play a part in their demise. So some of them tormented and taunted him and finally bound and betrayed him. They bound him with a silken cord made of magical strands—the sound of a cat's paw, hairs of a maiden's beard, roots of a mountain, dreams of a bear, breath of a fish and the spit of a bird. When Fenris breaks those bonds, the old Norse Gods and Asgard, home of the gods, will be destroyed. Odin will die as atonement for the deceptions and destructiveness of the Aesir and humans. But the sons of Fenris and the other wolves will cross the Rainbow Bridge and survive.

Wolves abound in Nordic traditions. In Viking belief, wolves chasing and devouring the sun and moon caused lunar and solar eclipses. The great wolf Hati constantly pursues the moon. The persistent Skoll chases the sun.

Norse references to wolves in myth and religion clearly indicate ties with shamanic religions. Vikings, Celts, Mycenaeans, Dorians, Anglos, Saxons and Germans are all descendants of Indo-European peoples with origins in the Caucasus region, where Europe and Asia meet. As hunting peoples, they had regular encounters with wolves, ravens and deer. They depended on cycles of the seasons and migrations of the herds for their very existence. Watching and learning from wolves and other denizens of forest, mountain and steppe was logical and wise.

Wolf as protector and teacher is a universal archetype. People who live close to predators and prey, like the old reindeer-herders of Siberia, the hunting societies of Mongolia, the proto-Celtic hunters and the ancestral Vikings, respected wolves because they saw their skills as persistent hunters and providers for the pack. No less a personage than Genghis Khan traced his ancestry back to the Siberian Blue Wolf. Genghis was both warrior and shaman. Turkic clans who traversed central Asia, migrated into Asia Minor and conquered Byzantium traced their ancestry to founders suckled and raised by wolves. They founded Turkish dynasties that ruled from Istanbul to the Red Sea, across North Africa and into central Europe. To this day, Turks honor the wolf. A nationalist political group in modern Turkey calls its members the Gray Wolves. For nomadic and warrior people, the wolf was a powerful totemic protector. These ancient memories linger.

In many cultures, the wolf was not only protector and teacher but also a guide between worlds, one who could travel between the World of the Living and the World of the Dead. Wolf was a guide through the spirit world and the transitions and transformations between life and death. This is fully in keeping with shamanic concepts.

Mystical medicine societies emerged in which Wolf was the central healing figure. In the Pacific Northwest, every winter during cycles of Winter Dances, when shorter days make people reflect on struggles between darkness and light and the inevitable transformations between life and death, ritual dancing reveals the incredible array of human, animal and mythic spirits populating the world. Among the traditional Makah, oceangoing whale hunters of the Olympic Peninsula, the Wolf Society captured new initiates at this time. Members of the healing fraternity left the village for several days. Through the aid of prayers and ritual masks, initiated members were transformed into wolves and entered the village. They carried away chosen new initiates back into the forests and through magical rituals transformed them into young wolves. After training and initiation, new members of the Wolf Society returned to their homes, with new responsibilities and obligations.

Winter was a sacred time of reflection and prayer for shamanic peoples. It was a time of sacred rites and initiations, echoes of which resound through antiquity and down to the modern era. Wolf as transformer and guide through the Underworld appears in the three faces of Hecate, the ancient Greek deity of magic and enchantment, who was worshipped at crossroads and portrayed as a goddess with three wolf heads looking into the past, present and future. Charon, the old ferryman who carried shades across the river Styx to Hades, had long, lupine ears. The association of the twin gods Artemis and Apollo with wolves and wolf-light evokes shamanic connections with healing, knowledge and rebirth. The maenads, beautiful women who sang and danced and drank wine to the point of divine ecstasy as sacred followers of Dionysus, were found in the company of wolves, deer, goats, satyrs and other denizens of the wild. Bacchanals and initiations of members into the Dionysiac and Orphic cults occurred during the Winter Solstice. The oldest mainland European civilization, the Celts, worshipped wolves as companions of the gods. In ancient Japan, Scythia and Persia, Wolf ranked high in traditional pantheons.

Since hunting was a primary focus of existence in archaic cultures, it is obvious why the wolf, with great hunting skills, acute hearing and strong family bonds expressed by vocalizations and body language, was respected and admired by humans. It is logical that creatures of such strength and intelligence would be incorporated into sacred traditions.

Scholars assert that with the development of farming and the domestication of livestock, people settled down and new cycles of belief and new traditions pushed out the old hunting deities and shamanistic intermediaries. It is more accurate to understand that changes in life-ways superimposed new forms of belief on old traditional ways, but old ways and old gods are never fully forgotten or lost. Like *pentimento* in frescoes and paintings, original foundations show through facades of pastoralism, agricultural revolutions and "civilization." There are myriad examples of this phenomenon.

In old traditions, diseases were believed to be caused by disharmony; by being out of balance with the world. Many things could cause such imbalance: witchcraft, jealousy and people who thought bad thoughts about others; vindictive spirits; individual irresponsibility—disregarding the animal, spirit and human realms and deliberately or accidentally violating taboos; or becoming obsessed with someone or something and not satisfying deep-seated desires. The shaman would be called in to diagnose the cause of illness. The same shaman or another shamanic specialist would then undertake a cure for the patient.

The shaman fasted and prayed in preparation for battling the forces manifesting in disease. In many societies, the shaman entered a sweat lodge, or sauna, as part of the ritual purification. The shaman, chosen by the spirits, undertook the journey between worlds to heal the afflicted. "Riding on the drum," calling on spirit helpers, using plants, herbs, paints and minerals, and voyaging through realms of Heaven, Earth and Underworld, the shaman would "doctor" the patient. Shamans continue their work in many places today. The procedures that Christian priests, preachers and Islamic *mullahs* use for casting out evil, "exorcisms," are identical to the old preparations for "shamanizing." While exorcisms are rare in modern times— when patient care is not holistic, but broken up into specialties that treat symptoms but not causes—they do still occur. Priests fast before exorcisms, they pray and bring sacred water and salt and ritual objects to the afflicted. They sing and pray their rituals, they order the evil spirits out of their patient in the name of their god. The main difference is that, after they have experienced a divine calling, priests are initated by other human beings, whereas shamans are taken directly by the Sacred. A cleric chooses his profession; a shaman is chosen.

Sometimes shamans were transformed with assistance from

spirit helpers, but it is irrelevant whether this was actual physical transformation or spiritual transformation through trance.
Old manifestations of shape-shifting exist in every literature.
In China and Japan, licentious foxes are said to change into
beautiful women and seduce men. Weretigers, werebears, and
werewolves populate the myths of Asia. Wereleopards, were-
jackals and werehyenas are common tales in Africa. In the
Americas, werejaguars, wereocelots, werelynxes, werecoyotes
and werewolves occur. Among the Celts, tales were told of
silkies, seals who transformed into beautiful people and married into human families. Enchanted children, like the Irish
Children of Lir, were transformed by magic into beautiful
swans. Viking tales tell of fabulous warriors, called *berserkers,*
changing into wolves and bears during battle and back to men
afterward. These are links to old shamanic tales.

Shamanism is the foundation of all religions. The belief in
World Above (Heaven), with Middle Ground (Earth) as the
domain of men and spirits and World Below (Underworld)
as home to powers of darkness and the Afterlife come straight
out of shamanic traditions. Companions of gods and spirits
like wolves and ravens, and the divine intermediaries who
assume human forms as prophets and saviors—all are from
ancient shamanic ways.

Wolf People: Lycanthropy

Among the most enduring tales of transformation, with tragic consequences in medieval Europe for both people and wolves, were the werewolf stories. In contrast to Hollywood, which has reduced the werewolf to a device to sell tickets and concessions, the medieval stories are truly tragic, dark and haunting. Scholars speculate that the transformation of Europe from paganism to Christianity changed the wolf from a tribal figure of nurturer and protector to one of cruel devourer and denizen of the Underworld. Others maintain that the cause was human society's shift from hunting to herding and farming. Both theories are simplistic. Not every pastoral or farming society hates wolves and seeks to exterminate them. Reindeer-herders of Siberia and Finland respect wolves and have lived beside them since the dawn of human experience. The Dineh of America's Great Southwest were the foremost pastoralists of North America. To this day, they respect wolves and fear members of secret societies called *yenotlochi,* "four-footed ones," who are said to change into wolves, coyotes and dogs and prowl at night, to peek and pry and do harm to others. The Dineh do not blame the animals for this evil human behavior. Hopis, descendants of the first human beings to walk the Colorado plateau, are farmers. They never tried to exterminate wolves or any other animal. Hatred of the wolf and attempts at wolf eradication point to something dark and evil in cultures that embrace destruction of life and the natural world.

The New Testament portrays Jesus as a shepherd protecting

lambs from wolves. Jesus exorcised demons from two poor
men who feared human company and lived among the dead
in the cemeteries of Gararenes on the Sea of Galilee. It is said
that these men howled like wolves before Jesus freed them
from their suffering. In both the Judaic Old Testament and the
Judeo-Christian New Testament, wolves are viewed as helpers
of Satan who carry away souls to the Underworld. Wolves killing and eating domesticated sheep was equated with evil, and
a sad disservice was done to both man and beast. Wolves were
portrayed as fanged, drooling, vindictive hounds of Hell, bent
on destruction. This image pervades Western European cultures to this day.

Werewolf images stalked medieval Europe. There were
many tales about them: Some said that wolfmen inherited
their powers from lycanthropic ancestors. Others said that
humans drinking from certain rivers caused the transformation. The most commonsense explanation of entrance into
lycanthropy said that one bitten by a rabid wolf became a
werewolf. In Italy, it was said that a boy conceived under a full
moon would become a werewolf. In some European legends,
only men become werewolves. In others, women and children
could become werewolves, too. Patrick, the bishop who Chris-
tianized Ireland, is said to have cursed an entire clan because
of their refusal to abandon their old gods for his god. He
doomed them to turn into wolves every seven years.

The word "werewolf" came from the Anglo-Saxon *wer,*
man and *wulf,* wolf. Germans called him *wahrwolf;* French, *le
loup-garou.* Despite connotations of evil, the hapless human

afflicted with this form of shape-shifting did not necessarily choose to enter the circle of werewolves. An old European rhyme stated:

> Even he who is pure of heart
> And says his prayers by night
> May become wolf
> When wolfbane blooms

According to European beliefs, werewolves could be identified while in human forms because they would have eyebrows that met, clawlike nails, and small, pointy ears, and the third finger on the left hand would be as long or longer than the second finger. In the *were* form, the person looked like a huge wolf with human facial features and clawed hands. It hunted by the light of the full moon and tore out its victim's throat, animal or human, and ate the raw flesh.

Britain's King John, brother of Richard Lionheart, the king forced by his nobles to sign the Magna Carta, the codification of English Common Law and the beginning of Constitutional Law, was rumored to have been a werewolf! King John died a year after he signed the Magna Carta. A Norman chronicler wrote that monks heard sounds coming from his grave and removed his body from consecrated ground. They feared the dead king was a werewolf and should not be buried on sacred ground. King John was not beloved by his subjects. It is likely the werewolf story was just an expression of popular discontent.

Just as there were many ways to become a werewolf, there were many ways to cure or destroy them. The *Malleus Malefi- carum,* "The Hammer of Witches," the most notorious of the old witch-hunting manuals, published in 1486, was used as a judicial casebook for the detection of witches and were- creatures. Written by two men, James Sprenger and Henry Kramer, it was used in Christian Europe for 300 years to tor- ment, torture and kill. Its victims were usually women who had money or property that someone else desired, or people who had retained pagan ways, including cultivation of medici- nal herbs and plants, and who believed in old gods and spirits. Many victims of this reign of terror were midwives, who prac- ticed herb lore and folk religion in their care of mothers and children. Some who were judicially tried and put to death were mentally ill, some were deformed people, others were just old people who lived alone and were considered "strange." Many animals such as dogs, cats, wolves, rabbits and other innocents met the same cruel fate. Witchcraft hysteria swept through Western Europe, and the Europeans exported it to their American colonies.

Detection and destruction of werewolves were also addressed in the *Malleus.* It is a document that displays the ignorance and cruelty of medieval Europe and illustrates the obsessive destruction wrought by men driven by fear while convinced that they held the keys to Absolute Truth.

The French seem to have been particularly plagued by werewolf mania. In France, taking three drops of blood from the loup-garou while it was in wolf form could defeat it. French-Canadians said that the wolf could be exorcised by calling out the name of Christ or calling the creature three times by its Christian name. Not all French remedies were so gentle. Accused werewolves were identified, tortured and killed; then they were hanged or burned or both.

European stories indicated that children were the favorite food of wolves and werewolves. In the 1600s, the tale of Little Red Riding Hood started to circulate. In 1697, it was written down and published by Perrault in his *Contes*. This story entered the canon of anti-wolf literature and causes grief for poor wolves even to this day. As recently as 1848, a lunar eclipse turned the moon the color of red blood. This instigated a rush of werewolf sightings throughout the Continent.

Not all of Christian Europe demonized wolves and werewolves. In some cases, wolves appear as protectors of the Church and destroyers of heresy. In 617, wolves and werewolves were alleged to have entered a monastery and killed several heretics. In Italy, people remember and discuss the siege of Loreto, when greedy soldiers from Urbino tried to take over the city to loot its sacred relics and treasures. In a miraculous intervention, packs of wolves attacked the Urbini and drove them away from Loreto.

Saints, Holy People, Kings and Wolves

Some saints were said to be protected by wolves. Tradition maintains that Irish Saint Albeus was suckled and raised by wolves. Since the old Celts considered wolves to be companions of their gods, it is no wonder that the new god and his saints would also enjoy their company.

One of the greatest medieval wolf stories is the tale of Francis d'Assisi and the Wolf of Gubbio. Gubbio is a beautiful walled city a few miles from Assisi in the hills of Umbria in Italy.

One day, Francis walked to Gubbio from his home in Assisi. After walking through the forests and into the central piazza, he was saddened to learn that Gubbio and its forests and hills were being terrorized by a huge wolf. The ferocious creature attacked and killed livestock and people alike, according to the residents. Everyone was afraid, and plans were afoot to gather a group of men together to kill the beast.

Francis felt pity for the people and sorrow for their fear. He felt compassion for the wolf, for surely no healthy and strong wolf would behave in such a way and live alone, away from a pack. "I will go to our Brother Wolf and meet with him," Francis sighed, and he walked into the forest.

The gentle man of Assisi, barefoot, unarmed and dressed in simple brown homespun, called the wolf to him. The huge creature walked toward him. Townspeople had followed Francis, and they hid in trees and underbrush to watch the fateful meeting. They feared for *Il Poverello,* "The Poor One." Francis made the Sign of the Cross and opened his arms to welcome the wolf. He said, "Brother Wolf, come here to me. Tell me what has hurt you so, that you hurt others."

The gigantic wolf walked up to Francis and placed his huge paws on the gentle man's shoulders and embraced him. He kissed Francis and hugged him.

"Brother Wolf, the people say you kill their animals and

you have killed some of them. It is wrong for you to attack God's creatures for no reason, and even men made in God's own image," Francis said. "People want to kill you, to send you to the gallows like a thief or an assassin. They cry out against you and call you an enemy. But it is my hope to make peace between you and them, my Brother."

As the citizens of Gubbio watched in fear, the wolf shook his massive head. He seemed to understand what Francis said. He bowed his head in deference to Francis, and in sorrow for past misdeeds. Then he wagged his tail and embraced Francis once again, and bowed playfully before him, accepting the saint's proposal.

Francis sat down with the huge wolf and held him in his arms. Despite the wolf's gigantic size, the holy man of Assisi felt the wolf's ribs through his beautiful fur. Francis understood the language of animals; he listened to the wolf as the wolf told him of the loss of his family at the hands of men, and of his loneliness and hunger. Francis held the wolf close to his heart, and then blessed him.

"Brother Wolf, since you wish to make peace, I promise you that as long as you live, the people of this region will give you food every day, so that you will no longer suffer from hunger. You will be welcome in their homes, so you will no longer suffer from being alone," Francis explained.

The lupine giant stood up on his hind legs and put his great paws in the saint's gentle hands. The smiling Francis held the wolf's paws and kissed him. The peace pact was sealed, to the astonishment of the onlookers.

"This wolf is not wicked," Francis announced. "This wolf is not evil. He is hungry. People killed his family. This wolf is lonely. He needs food and love."

The people of Gubbio were ashamed that cruelty had led to cruelty, and they promised to care for the wolf. From that day, the wolf was tame and gentle. He protected the livestock and children of Gubbio. The people fed him well every day. They welcomed him into their homes and gave him a warm bed and clean water. He lived for many, many years. And when the great and noble beast died from old age, he was mourned and missed in Gubbio. The people built a chapel on the spot outside the walls of Gubbio where Francis and the wolf had met. To honor the wolf and Francis, they buried the wolf beneath the altar. They made a woodcut memorializing the meeting. The woodcut shows Francis and the wolf embracing, with the wolf's great paws on the saint's shoulders and Francis kissing the wolf on the top of his gigantic head, between his two pointed ears.

Some maintain that the story of Francis and the wolf is symbolic of the saint's mission of peace and reconciliation and the power of God. If God is love; if God is respect for other beings and a love of Nature and the cosmos, then God has no greater messenger than Francis and no story more beautiful than that of Francis and the Wolf of Gubbio.

But there is more to this story than symbolism. A few years ago, during restoration of the Wolf Chapel near Gubbio, as the archeologists were working on the altar, a part of the altar crumbled and revealed the bones of a huge wolf. The Wolf of Gubbio was far more than an allegory. He was as real as the gentle man who loved him and all life, so very long ago.

Modern Manifestations

Shamanic echoes of the power of Wolf reverberate today. In Siberia, a land which has finally been freed from hundreds of years of domination by invaders—first Christian Czarist Russians and then the Red Russians, the shamans are now old and few, but the spirit poles have returned to their rightful places before family homes, and drumming and singing are no longer secret affairs. In the Western hemisphere, Euro-Americans can no longer legally persecute indigenous peoples for their beliefs. In the United States and Canada, tribal populations have survived their nadir, their low point. Tribes that survived the onslaught of invasion, disease and land-grabbing are gaining in numbers. Most Indian people are under the age of thirty-five, so there will be many more children.

The prophecy of a Paiute holy man, Wovoka, of Indian population recovery, the promised return of buffalo, elk and wolf, has come true. While not in the numbers of the past, at least they have survived. Native peoples have survived because of strength of will, determination and their relationship with land. The American people demanded the protection of the buffalo, the return of wolves to some of their old lands and protection of endangered land and species. True, the world has changed. Much remains to be done, but old religious ways are returning, and in many places they never went away. The power of Wolf remains and manifests itself in interesting ways.

A few years ago, in the forests of the Chippewa, a young Ojibway man and his girlfriend ventured out for dinner on a frosty New Year's Eve. The young man promised both sets of parents to have his girlfriend home before midnight. The couple enjoyed a leisurely dinner at a restaurant, while outside temperatures dropped to twenty-five degrees below zero. By ten o'clock, the pair decided that they should head to the girl's house. They left the restaurant and jumped into the boy's pickup truck.

As they headed home on a remote stretch of forest road, the truck's engine sputtered and died. All attempts to restart the motor failed. It was getting closer to midnight, and the boy didn't want to get into trouble with the families. The pair had passed a house about a mile back, and the boy decided that he should walk there and use the telephone to call his family. Fortunately, there were blankets and candles in the truck. He and his date agreed that she would wait in the vehicle while he walked for help.

The young man was inadequately dressed for the deep winter cold. Although it was winter, he had not anticipated a midnight walk. The mile turned into two miles. Finally, he spotted the house lights and walked up the driveway. He knocked on the door and waited.

After several minutes, a cranky old man cracked the door open. "What do you want?" the man asked. The teenager explained his dilemma. "Sir, may I please use your telephone to call my parents? My truck broke down and I need help."

"No, you can't," snarled the mean old man. "And get out of here. Get off my property." He slammed the door.

The young man was speechless. Desperate and disheart-
ened, he slowly turned to start the long trudge across cold and
snow to his girl and the comparative safety of the truck. In
order to save time, he decided to cut across country back to
the vehicle. As he walked, he felt something following him.
He saw a shadowy form slip through the trees. This made him
nervous. As he walked through the snow, he heard other footsteps crunching in the snow. He heard breathing that was not
his own. But worse, he was becoming weak and sleepy from
exposure to the extreme cold.

He knew that he would freeze to death if he stopped walking, and the following shadow was the least of his worries.
Try as he might, he could not keep going. He collapsed and
blacked out. When he awoke, he found a gigantic wolf beside
him, nudging him. He did not sense danger from the majestic
creature. He put his arms around the wolf's neck. The wolf
breathed warm breath into the boy's face. The wolf's body heat
helped the boy revive. The wolf helped him walk and guided
him to within sight of the truck. "Thank you, thank you," the
boy whispered to the wolf. When they were near the truck, the
wolf nudged the youngster and then turned and vanished into
the woods.

The young man stumbled into the arms of his girlfriend
and she wrapped him up in blankets. "What was that with
you?" the girl asked. "It looked like a wolf." The boy stam-
mered a reply, "He—he saved me. He was a wolf."

He told her that all they could do was bundle up and wait
for help. The next morning, passing motorists stopped and
helped them. They asked the couple what they needed. The

pair asked if they could call for help. The motorists drove several miles away to the nearest gas station and telephoned the families. The boy's uncles were already searching for them. One of them arrived with a tow truck and took them home.

The boy told his family the amazing story. Then, his grandmother said, "You are Wolf Clan of the Ojibway. Sometimes, they come and help their relations."

Dineh (Navajos) of the Four Corners region of the Great Southwest have a different relationship with wolves. They are Athabascans, descendants of great hunters and shamans. They believe that they entered this world after traveling through a series of worlds beneath the earth. They learned from their journeys and met the Holy People, their gods. Dineh ancestors, First Man and First Woman, emerged from a lake near Mount Hesperus and Mount Blanca, in what is now the Four Corners area of Colorado, New Mexico, Arizona and Utah. In those days, the Dineh were hunters. They carved out a homeland for themselves, bounded by four sacred Mountains, Tsinajiin (Mount Blanca), Tsoodzil (Mount Taylor), Dook'oo'sliid, (San Francisco peaks) and Dibe'nitsaa (Mount Hesperus). They built their homeland following instructions from the Holy People and the divine daughter of First Man and First Woman, Changing Woman.

Changing Woman taught the Dineh how to walk in balance; how to live in harmony. Living in balance on our Mother Earth is called *hozho,* Beauty. All life was respected, and many things were avoided because of their sacred power. Animals like *Mauii,* Coyote, and *Mauii Tso,* Wolf, were representatives

of gods. They were messengers and treated with respect. Since
their origins, Dineh have been plagued with jealous evildoers
who gain power by hurting others. These people may study
to be *hatalii,* singers and medicine people, and acquire the
ability to tap into the power of Nature. They join with other
witches to cause illness, to hoard wealth and hurt others.
They do not walk in Beauty. To do their nefarious deeds,
they don the skins of coyotes and wolves and prowl around
at night, spying on their enemies and making people sick with
corpse dust.

Dineh call these wicked people *yenotlochi,* "four-footed
ones," because they assume canine forms when they prowl.
Sometimes they are called Skinwalkers. Because of their fear
of witches and respect for sacred messengers, Dineh regard all
coyotes and wolves with a mixture of fear and respect.

Navajo Ranger Jon Dover explained that wolves and
coyotes are innocent of evil. Dover is Dineh, but he is also
a descendant of Cheyenne survivors of Sand Creek. He has
special interests in protection of archeological and cultural
resources. "The Skinwalkers are kind of like *ninjas,*" Dover
explained. "They wear those skins and have delivery systems of
poisons to make people sick. They kill a member of their own
family in order to join the society. They are wicked people who
blackmail people and abuse power."

With the coming of the Spanish to the Southwest, the
Holy People delivered sheep, goats, cattle and horses to the
Dineh, who became mounted warriors and herdsmen. They
became the finest pastoralists in the Western Hemisphere.

In the Navajo Way, people are responsible for taking good care of their livestock. If a wolf takes a sheep, it is not the fault of the wolf. The wolf is only behaving like a wolf. The shepherd is the guilty one—for not paying close attention and protecting the flock. If too much predation occurs, a combination of negligence and disharmony must be the cause. A hatalii will be consulted to determine the cause of the problem. A ceremony, or "sing," will be held to bring the shepherd, flock and family back into harmony.

All the clan relatives, friends and community will come to the sing to help restore balance. At the conclusion of the ceremonies, the land, people, animals and plants will benefit. Balance will be restored. All will walk again in Beauty.

Among the Sammi (called Laplanders by Europeans) who are reindeer-herders and salmon-fishers of the Baltic and Finland, the wolf is associated with amber, one of the region's most ancient exports. Some of the world's finest amber comes from this part of the world. The old amber trail tied the archaic Baltic to cultures of the Mediterranean, the British Isles and Asia Minor, long before the Bronze Age.

The Sammi, whose ancestors migrated west from Siberia thousands of years ago, maintain that there is a sacred connection between the glittering gold color of wolf eyes and amber. The amber eyes of the wolf are linked to celestial events—comets, "falling stars" and lightning. The full moon is a special ally of the wolf, and both moon and wolf are sacred to the Sammi. Among the Sammi, it is said that when wolves encounter amber, they make prayers to it and kiss the fossilized resin to gain strength and power and communicate with the sacred powers of the sky.

Belief in animal spirits and guides survives today. Circumpolar peoples, the tribes of the Pacific Northwest and other indigenous people have held fast to their beliefs. In regions where they have been able to retain even small pieces of their original homeland, the link between land, identity and survival is unbreakable. In 1999, students at the Selkirk Elementary School of Whitehorse in Canada's Yukon Territories wrote down stories they had learned from family members and drew pictures to illustrate them.

In one story, retold by a student named Brenen Wolf, we learn how wolves learned to howl.

> When Grandpa set camp and before his grandchildren went to bed, a wolf howled. Then Grandpa said, "Let me tell you how Wolf learned to howl. . . . Long ago, Wolf saw this beautiful full moon. The next morning, Raven saw Wolf sad and droopy. Raven called to Wolf, 'Wolf, why are you sad and droopy?'
>
> " 'Wolf said, "Raven, I wanted to say something or anything to the full moon . . .'
>
> " 'Why don't you howl to the full moon?' asked Raven. Then Wolf said, 'I can't howl to the full moon because I don't know how to howl.'
>
> "Raven changed into a wolf and showed Wolf how to howl. The next full moon, Wolf tried and tried and tried to howl. He tried for two weeks. Later, he asked Raven

again, 'How do you howl?' Raven showed him one more time, then flew away. Wolf tried to howl to the next full moon. Then he heard a howl. It was him. The next morning, Wolf thanked Raven.

"So that's how Wolf learned to howl," said Grandpa. Grandpa put out the fire and everyone went to bed.

Leah Wolf retold the story of how Wolf learned to hunt. This is what she wrote:

One night Grandfather and the children gathered around the fire. Grandfather said, "Tonight, I am going to tell you the legend of how Wolf learned to hunt. One day in a far away village there lived a wolf. There was a problem . . . Wolf didn't like to eat anything except berries. He didn't even like eating meat. [It was] the first day of Winter. Wolf went out to pick berries. He could not find them. Wolf started digging, but when he found the berries they were frozen solid. Wolf went back to Raven to complain.

"Raven said he was sorry about the berries, but there was nothing he could do, that was the way Winter was. That night, Raven couldn't sleep because he felt sorry for Wolf, so Raven went to the Spirit of the Forest. Raven told all about what had happened with Wolf. The wise old Spirit suggested that Raven teach Wolf how to hunt. Raven thanked the Spirit of the Forest and left to start training Wolf.

"The next day, Wolf and Raven started training.
It wasn't going too well at first, but once Wolf figured it
out, he had a storage of meat. He didn't know what it
was for. So Wolf . . . asked Raven what it was for. Raven
answered that it was for Wolf to eat. Wolf still didn't
understand—why would he want to eat food that came
from animals? Raven explained to Wolf that it was the
way life was. Wolf did not understand why he had to eat
meat—but Raven told him that it was the way of life,
and because he would die if he didn't eat the meat."

Grandfather said that was the end of my story, and
now it was time for bed. . . .

These stories, remembered and retold by children, are part
of an unbroken chain of enduring belief, myth and legend
going back thousands of years to the dawn of human consciousness. Thus the power of Wolf endures.

There are many modern manifestations of belief in wolf
power, but one of the most important manifestations is wolf
survival. There was a time when wolf and men willingly shared
the world. Once, the two species, human and wolf, were the
most widely distributed mammals on the planet. But how did
wolves come to be, and what has been their relationship with
humans and other creatures? And what happened to make
so many men hate wolves and persecute them to the edge of
extinction?

Wolf Origins & Behaviors

*W*olves emerged in Eurasia about a million years ago during the Pleistocene epoch. Like all mammals, wolves evolved from small ratlike insect-eaters who entered the fossil record during the Cretaceous period. Some 60 million years ago, in the Paleocene epoch, meat-eating mammals developed. This order is called *Carnivora.* The early meat-eaters were called *miacids.* They were common ancestors to dogs, bears, seals, cats, hyenas, weasels and civets. About 20 million years ago, in the Miocene period, miacids split into two groups, *Feloidea* and *Canoidea.* Canines developed from Canoidea. Cats evolved from Feloidea. Wolves, jackals and coyotes evolved from a weasel-like animal called *Tomarctus,* who walked the earth on short legs 15 million years ago. From the stubby Tomarctus evolved the ancestor of modern canids, *Cynodictis.* These were successful animals, and their line split into many different species and migrated throughout the planet. Some species crossed from Siberia to North America across the Bering land bridge during the last glaciation. These hunting families were the direct ancestors of today's New World wolves, coyotes and foxes. Gray wolves and red foxes exist in both the

Old and the New World because their ancestors walked between the two, following game.

About 400,000 years ago, a giant canid called *Canis dirus,* the dire wolf, coexisted with the ancestors of today's wolf. Its physique was stockier and more robust than that of modern wolves. Its enormous jaws crushed bone easily, and it was even more powerful than our *Canis lupus.* California's La Brea tar pits, near modern Los Angeles, have given up over 3,600 dire wolf carcasses. According to the extant fossil record, this animal became extinct 10,000 years ago.

Scientists categorize life in order to better understand origins and relationships. Taxonomy is the branch of biology that classifies and names living things. Each species is given a two-part name, which consists of the species name and a specific description.

Scientists use these classified names in their publications. The most common wolf species is the gray wolf. These wolves survive today in North America, Asia and parts of Europe. According to the organizing system developed in the eighteenth century by the Swedish botanist Linnaeus, this is the taxonomy of the gray wolf:

Kingdom: *Animalia*
Phylum: *Chordata*
Subphylum: *Vertebreta*
Class: *Mammalia*
Subclass: *Eutheria*
Order: *Carnivora*
Suborder: *Caniforma*

Family: *Canidae*
Genus: *Canis*
Species: *lupus*

A genus is a group of related creatures. The gray wolf, *Canis lupus,* is closely related to the red wolf, *Canis rufus,* who survive today in very small numbers in the southeastern United States. Jackals and Abyssinian wolves are in the same genus, as are all other wolves, dogs and foxes—all are in the same biological "family," the *Canidae,* dogs. Canidae are meat-eaters, and this links them with cats and bears, so all are in the order *Carnivora.* Similar orders are placed in larger groups. The wolf has fur and provides milk for her young, so, like the cat, the platypus and the dolphin, the wolf is in the *Mammalia* class. Similar classes are grouped into phyla—the wolf is in the *Chordata* phylum. Phyla are parts of kingdoms, and the wolf is in the kingdom *Animalia.*

Wolves are the largest members of the canine or dog family. They can weigh between 60 and 200 pounds and measure between 24 and 36 inches from ground to shoulder and between 60 and 72 inches from head to tail. Males are usually larger than females. Northern wolves are usually larger and heavier than southern wolves. For example, some Arctic and Canadian MacKenzie wolves can weigh up to 200 pounds; a Mexican wolf, indigenous to the desert Southwest, usually weighs no more than 75 pounds. The smallest surviving wolf is the Arabian wolf, indigenous to the Arabian peninsula and Sinai; they weigh from 20 to 30 pounds.

Wolf fur is called *pelage.* Wolves have a double layer of fur:

the top layer is thick, oily guard hair designed to protect the wolf against moisture—water, snow and dampness. The second layer is a thick, insulating undercoat that keeps the wolf warm. Wolves are so well insulated that snow will not melt on their fur. Wolves lose almost no body heat through their fur. The bushy tail of a wolf serves many purposes. When a wolf is cold, it will wrap up in its tail, with the tail covering the nose, to keep its nostrils and face warm. Wolves also use their tails to communicate and have an elaborate body language and vocalization system.

Wolves come in many colors and variations of colors— white, black, golden, cinnamon, gray, silver, brown. Usually, wolf hairs are not one standard color, but a combination of banded colors. This banding is called *agouti,* after the huge South American rodent with the colorful fur coat. A pigment called *eumelanin,* which is stimulated by enzymes that turn it on, causes the multicolored strand of each wolf hair to turn on and off during the hair-growth cycle, thus causing color banding on the fur. Many wolves have lighter coloration, called "masks," around the eyes and cheek areas.

Seasons affect wolf coloring. The boldest coloration appears in winter. In summer, during shedding, coat colors fade. Life cycles can also affect wolf coloration. Cubs often shift in coloration from birth through adulthood. For example, Arctic wolf cubs are born a beige or light-brown color, but as they grow up, their coats turn white. Timber wolf cubs are usually born brown, but they turn grayer as they grow up.

Wolves are built for running. They hunt by stalking, then

running the prey down and making a quick kill. They are persistence hunters and can travel up to 70 miles in one day. Wolves can run as fast as 40 miles per hour for short distances. Wolves have long, agile legs. They walk on their toes, an adaptation called *digitigrade*. Their claws are nonretractable, and their tracks range in size from 3.5 to 4 inches wide and 4.5 to 5 inches long.

Wolves' heads are shaped by a long, narrow skull with a bone at the top of the skull called a sagittal crest. The jaw muscles connect at the sagittal crest to give them a powerful downward bite. Wolves have large eye sockets on the front of the skull. Wolf cubs are born with blue eyes, but their eyes change color as they grow up. Wolf eyes can be many colors— many hues of yellow, amber and green.

Wolves have forty-two teeth in their long, narrow mouths. Their four canine teeth can be up to two inches long. Such long, sharp teeth enable the predator to bite through the toughest hide. Two canines are in the upper jaw and two are in the lower. Wolves have four carnassials, molarlike teeth toward the rear of the mouth. These are meat-shearers. Wolves have small incisors, which they use to grasp food. Many people envision wolves as meat-eating predators routinely bringing down huge game animals like musk oxen and moose on a daily basis. They do not realize that wolves are opportunistic feeders and will eat just about anything they can catch; as a group, they work to bring down big game, but this is not a daily event. Wolves eat moose, deer, caribou (reindeer), elk, bighorn sheep, antelope, rabbits, squirrels, birds, mice, fruits, nuts, grasses, eggs—all types of things. Many times I have observed wolves collecting nuts and enjoying them. I have seen them eat blueberries, moose berries and huckleberries with relish. I have seen them suffer bee stings to get wild honey. Biologists say that vegetation is essential in wolf diets to ensure proper nutrient balance and provide roughage. They maintain that wolves generally get enough vegetable matter from eating the stomachs of their prey, but they will supplement this by "grazing."

Wolves have extraordinary senses of smell and hearing. They detect prey by scent, sound and sight. They study a herd before a hunt. They watch carefully to detect weak, old, sick or very young animals. They use their noses to detect signs of infection in prey urine or feces. Wolves can smell infection and sickness and identify such an animal as easy prey. Wolves stalk their prey. Once a potential meal is identified, the pack splits into smaller groups and surrounds its target.

Large game—like moose, buffalo, elk or musk ox—is dangerous for wolves. Horns and antlers are sharp and deadly. A kick from a moose hoof or a blow from an ox can kill or cripple a wolf. Wolves try to attack the rear of the big animals to get the blood flowing. Then, they try to make the animal run, so it will collapse from exhaustion and blood loss. A weakened animal does not suffer long—it may collapse from exhaustion, be taken down and have its neck broken by wolves, have a heart attack or die from shock. After the kill, the head wolves, the *alpha pair,* eat first. The heart, liver and entrails are devoured quickly. Each wolf eats in the order of its rank in the pack. After the group finishes eating, little remains except hooves, horns and a few large bones. If anything more remains, the wolves will return to finish it later, but foxes, coyotes, vultures, ravens, magpies and other birds and insects usually finish up the carcass.

Wolves kill smaller prey like mice, rabbits and birds by breaking the backbone. An individual wolf takes such small game.

An old and sacred relationship exists between hunted and hunter. Wolves and game dance an ancient dance; predator and prey move in archaic rhythms—the dance of death, the dance of life. Each is dependent on the other. The wolf needs the meat of the game to survive. Herds need the strength of the wolf to remain strong and healthy. Wolves cull the weak. They shorten the suffering of the sick. They help the strong become stronger. Wolves kill only when they are hungry. They do not kill for fun or for sport. They do not torture their prey. They do not kill for trophies.

Even when wolves are not hungry, they react with joy when they see game. Wolves I worked with became very excited and their faces filled with happiness whenever they scented or saw buffalo, deer and even cattle. Biologists speculate that deer, elk and caribou herds have been evolutionarily shaped by their ancient relationships with wolves.

To be healthy and strong, wolves need about three to ten pounds of meat and three quarts of water daily from food or drink. Wolves do not consume huge hooved animals at every meal. Only about one in ten hunts of bigger animals is successful, so wolves binge when they eat. They can gobble as much as twenty pounds in a single feeding—hence the term "to wolf down food." There is a substantive survival advantage to eating food quickly: no competitor can take it from you that way.

Some people still blame wolves for changes in deer populations. This is a fallacy—an old wives' tale. Wolves take less than one-half of one percent of the total population of game animals. Human hunters are estimated to kill about ten percent of game animals. More game is killed by people driving cars than by wolves eating them. Disease and starvation and habitat loss kill more game animals than do wolves. As noted conservationist Aldo Leopold observed, areas where there are no predators become lands of waste, starvation and desolation for deer and other species. If wolves and other predators are not there to hunt, elk and deer populations explode and there is no food. Suffering and death result.

Too many human hunters go into the woods to kill not because they are hungry, but because they want a trophy. Thus, they kill the strongest and the most beautiful and leave the sick and the weak to suffer. This is the opposite of the natural cycle.

Some people maintain that wolves attack and kill livestock and are a threat to the cattle industry. Wolves will eat whatever is weak. It is true that they have taken livestock in areas where their natural prey is gone or hard to find. In some cases, livestock has been easy and convenient for wolves, so they make a kill. However, wolves account for less than one percent of all livestock deaths. The conservation group, Defenders of Wildlife, compensate livestock growers with full market value for any animal killed and eaten by wolves. The United States Fish and Wildlife Service keeps a close eye on areas where reintroduced wolf packs and livestock interact, and the agency eliminates entire packs of wolves if they become livestock predators. The facts are that feral and pet dogs are responsible for most livestock attacks. Yes, the same family hound or poodle who enjoys kibble and plays with the children can form a pack with other dogs and go into a frenzy and kill cattle, sheep, and even people. Wolves kill to eat, and they don't go into this frenzy. Wolves' hunting is calculated and deliberate. And again, the human factor enters the equation: Cars hit more cattle every year than are killed by wolves.

Wolves evolved, multiplied and developed a global niche. They lived in extended families, called packs. Their habitat included tundra, grasslands, fir forests, broadleaf forests, jungles, swamps, deserts and mountains. The wolf homeland extended from Eurasia into North America, including what are now Canada, the United States and Mexico. Wolf populations extended into Europe, the Middle East, the Arabian peninsula, India, Tibet and Nepal. Their range was the largest of all mammals except one. Only modern humans—*Homo sapiens,* the "wise man"—had a greater range. In the early days of humankind, man and wolf walked the same territories and lived in peace together. But eventually, civilized humans turned against wolves and tried to exterminate them. They almost succeeded.

Today's wolf range is drastically reduced from the days when men and wolves shared the world in harmony. Wolves survive in parts of Canada, Alaska, Minnesota, Michigan, Wisconsin, Montana, Idaho, Wyoming and a few other states. Europeans nearly eradicated wolves, but a few survive in the Abruzzi Mountains of Italy, in Spain, Romania, Finland, Greece, Turkey and Russia. Interestingly, the gray wolf is doing well in Greece, where several packs live in the mountainous north. The Greek government estimates that between 500 and 700 wolves live on the upper mainland.

A pack was recently introduced into the forests of Mount Parnis, about an hour's drive north of Athens. The wolves seem to be adapting well, according to Greek wolf-watcher Michael Odysseus Yakoumakis and the Hellenic Forestry Office. Greek shepherds, descendants of people who have lived in the Balkans for millennia, maintain that they learned to live with wolves through vigilance—paying close attention to their flocks and their dogs—and that if a wolf takes a sheep, it is due to negligence on the part of the shepherd and his dog, not to a transgression by the wolf. "After all," explains Christou Samarina, a venerable and hoary Vlach shepherd, "everyone must eat, and God made us all."

Vlach shepherds say that despite bounties paid for wolves since antiquity, Greeks have never made a systematic attempt to exterminate them. "We adapt to the land, we use free-range grazing," one shepherd explained. "We learn how to protect our sheep; we know the land, we know where there are water and springs, we know where to expect wolves. Somehow, we all work it out, our sheepdogs, the wolves and ourselves."

Wolves were persecuted in Europe until recent years. The

English killed their last free wolf in 1486. The Scots destroyed
their forests and killed their last wolves in 1743. The British-
occupied Irish killed their last wolf in 1770. The only known
surviving wolves in Scandinavia are in Finland and Norway.
Interestingly, these wolves share lands in the north with other
persecuted tribes, the Sammi. To this day, many Sammi survive by herding reindeer and living a semi-nomadic lifestyle.
Sammi people do not hate wolves. They respect them and
have lived with them and the reindeer for thousands of years.

India's wolves, made beloved to the world by the writings
of British colonialist Rudyard Kipling and his *Jungle Book* and
Just So Stories, needed the forests of the subcontinent to survive. Although tales of sightings occasionally surface, India's
"Free People," as Kipling's wolves described themselves, are
now extinct.

As a result of European incursions, wolves were decimated
in North America. The litany of terror and brutality against
wolves by humans is horrific, vast and bloody. Writers like
Barry Lopez (*Of Wolves and Men* and *Arctic Dreams*) have described it. Two books released in 1944, Young and Goldman's
The Wolves of North America; and Adolph Murie's *The Wolves
of Mount McKinley,* include aspects of the decimation. The
bounty rolls of the United States and the Canadian federal
governments document it. It is sadistic and tragic. The question one asks after reviewing this history of carnage is "Why?"
Why people acted with such cruelty remains a mystery. For
some, it was misguided concern for deer, moose and other
game, due to ignorance and misunderstanding of Nature's

systems. They did not realize how the number of prey controls the number of predators and not vice versa. For others, the new invaders, it was ignorance coupled with desire to protect their livestock herds while imposing their own changes on the land. For others, it was the sheer joy of killing—wolf, bear, buffalo, even other human beings, including Native Americans and anyone "different" from themselves. Euro-Americans were determined to destroy these others, until former killers like Aldo Leopold began to realize the horrors being perpetrated in the name of progress. Leopold, one of the fathers of modern environmentalism, wrote about his epiphany in *The Sand County Almanac,* first released in 1948. The dawning of his awakening to Nature's reality occurred deep in the Gila wilderness of New Mexico, at the foot of a river:

> We saw what we thought was a doe fording the torrent, her breast awash in white water. When she climbed the bank toward us and shook out her tail, we realized our error: it was a wolf. A half-dozen others, evidently grown pups, sprang from the willows and all joined in a welcoming mêlée of wagging tails and playful maulings. . . . In those days we had never heard of passing up a chance to kill a wolf. . . . When our rifles were empty, the old wolf was down, and a pup was dragging a leg into impassable slide-rocks. We reached the old wolf in time to watch a fierce green fire dying in her eyes. I realized then, and have known ever since, that there was something new to me in those eyes—something known only to her and to the mountain. I was young then, and

full of trigger-itch; I thought that because fewer wolves
meant more deer, that no wolves would mean hunters'
paradise. But after seeing the green fire die, I sensed that
neither the wolf nor the mountain agreed with such a
view. (*Leopold, 1948*)

Leopold was involved with the federal extirpation of wolves
and other predators from the West. The horror of those days
and the imbalances they created made Leopold realize that
civilized attitudes were wrong.

I have watched the face of many a newly wolfless
mountain, and seen the south-facing slopes wrinkle with
a maze of new deer trails. I have seen every edible bush
and seedling browsed, first to anemic desuetude, and
then to death. . . . In the end the starved bones of the
hoped-for deer herd, dead of its own too-much, bleach
with the bones of the dead sage, or molder under the
high-lined junipers. (*Leopold, 1948*)

Perhaps the groundbreaking book of the twentieth century
that revolutionized popular American attitudes toward wolves
was Lois Crisler's 1958 masterwork, *Arctic Wild.* In 1956, Lois
and her husband, Herb Crisler, accepted an assignment from
Walt Disney to photograph caribou migrations for the film
White Wilderness. As caribou are a foundation of the Arctic
ecological system, this assignment led them to study related
wildlife in the region. At that time, Alaska truly was the last
great American frontier, and the Crislers lived in harsh con-

ditions, close to their photographic subjects in the remote
Brooks Range and Arctic tundra. From direct observation, the
Crislers realized that wolves were essential to healthy caribou
herds. Lois called wolves the "wild shepherds of the caribou,"
and "gentle-hearted predators." They ended up raising orphaned wolf cubs and came to understand that stories of
wolf cruelty and viciousness were untrue.

"Wolves are . . . gentle-hearted," Crisler wrote. "They are
not just feisty, fighting animals. . . . Wolves have what it takes
to live together in peace. . . . In a reasonable world, these
peaceful predators would be the most cherished object of
study by our race, trying to unlearn war. Why then do people
hate wolves and seek to exterminate them? . . . It takes a psychiatrist to say. . . . Wolves are not a menace to the wilds but
orgies of wolf hate are. Wolves themselves are a balance wheel
of nature."

Crisler's observations and life with wolves led her to love
and respect them, to distinguish the wolf of Nature's reality
from the savage wolf of European tales. Her observations created a sensation when *Arctic Wild* was released. By living with
the caribou, the wolf, the fox, the tundra and the mountains,
Crisler came to realize what her ancestors of so long ago had
known: that all life is sacred. In a letter to one of her editors
written while working on the sequel to her first book, *Captive
Wild,* Crisler wrote that she was afraid to admit this. "I dare
not say it in the book, but I have a sense of holiness about
wild nature, in spite of its sometimes dreadful aspects . . . I
want to find some way of expressing this feeling acceptably."

Apparently, in the 1950s it was not socially acceptable to

expound on the divine aspects of Sacred Nature. People es-
pousing such beliefs and voicing them were viewed as "kooks,"
unless they were Hindus, Native Americans or foreigners; and
then such views were regarded as "exotic" and "quaint." But
Crisler's work, Leopold's published musings and *Silent Spring,*
Rachel Carson's indictment of DDT pesticide, galvanized the
American public. The writings of Leopold, Carson and Crisler,
combined with the yearnings of generations of Americans for
preservation and protection, sparked a new environmental
consciousness and radicalism in the United States—a consciousness that is spreading globally. No longer is it socially
unacceptable to speak of love and reverence for the natural
world. Among indigenous peoples, it never was embarrassing.

These values have been reawakened, and the conscious
struggle to protect and retain natural balance is engaged
against forces of overpopulation, psychotic capitalism and deliberate destruction of the world for economic and political
gain. The outcome is unknown and the balance is precarious.
To people who love and respect wilderness and maintain that
wild places and creatures are necessary for global survival, the
wolf is a consummate symbol. What behaviors did Crisler,
Leopold and others see that opened their eyes and made them
love a predator so maligned by so many? It is to wolf ethology,
wolf behavior, that we now turn.

Life with the Pack

Rudyard Kipling, best known for his romantic fantasy, *The
Jungle Book,* which featured the adventures of an orphan boy

rescued and reared by wolves in the jungles of old India, showed great insight into wolves when he wrote:

> Now this is the Law of the Jungle—as old and as true as
>   the sky;
> And the Wolf that shall keep it may prosper, but the Wolf
>   that shall break it must die.
> As the creeper that girdles the tree-trunk the Law runneth
>   forward and back—
> For the strength of the Pack is the Wolf, and the strength of
>   the Wolf is the Pack.

In the wild, wolves have a lifespan of about seven to ten years. Wolves reach sexual maturity at age two, but they rarely mate at that young an age, if ever. That privilege is retained by the head wolves, called the alpha male and alpha female. Wolves live in family groups called packs. A pack consists of anywhere between three to forty members.

The alpha pair, their offspring and sometimes the alpha pair's brothers and sisters, make up a pack. There is a strict hierarchy in a wolf pack. This hierarchy is enforced regarding eating, mating and even howling. Alphas eat first at a kill, even if an *omega*—the lowest-ranking member of the pack, has made the kill. Pack members wait for permission from the alphas before eating. Sometimes, the omega has to wait to eat until after every other wolf has eaten. To the outside observer, the strict hierarchy may seem cruel, but it preserves order, and wolves go up and down the social ladder. Each wolf knows its place, and each provides for the pack. Usually, the omega is a comedian and peacemaker for the other wolves. Some biologists call the omega a "Cinderella" wolf. If an omega survives, it may rise in the pack and even achieve alpha status. This has been observed by biologists and was the case with a pack in Yellowstone Park.

Often, other wolves pick on the Cinderella wolf. By doing this, they also relieve tension in the family. Wolves bond closely with one another, and they play much more than they fight. The Cinderella wolf is a consummate diplomat, the one who often arbitrates in disputes between pack members by doing something funny to distract the pack or bowing down to invite play or wrestling.

Wolf mating season is usually between January and March. The farther north a pack is, the later the breeding season. Mating is a major event in the life of a wolf pack, and the alpha pair makes no secret about their activities. Then the mother-to-be prepares a den. Just before the birth, she enters the den and allows no wolf to enter, not even her mate, until some time after her cubs are born. After a gestation of about sixty-five days, the mother gives birth to between three and fourteen cubs. Each cub weighs no more than a pound. Cubs are born blind and helpless, with tiny little bodies, tiny heads, closed eyes and tiny pink feet. The mother suckles her cubs and is dependent on food left for her by pack members. She will stay close to her young for weeks before allowing them to leave the den and meet the rest of the family. About two weeks after they are born, the cubs open their eyes. The mother suckles them for a minimum of four weeks and gradually introduces them to other foods—brought to them by other wolves and regurgitated for them.

While the cubs are in the den, the other females go through what is called a pseudo-pregnancy: they behave as if they are pregnant and even lactate—but they don't whelp. This is an excellent survival strategy: In the event that the mother dies, the "aunties" can nurse the young ones. These females also help nurse the cubs after the mother allows them to meet the other pack members.

Cubs start getting their first teeth when they are about three weeks old. By four weeks, they are curious about the world outside the den, and they are allowed to wander out and meet their family. Tremendous anticipation and excitement sweeps a pack when the young ones come out. Wolves love cubs—in fact, they love young things of all types. They will accept young puppies as well as their own cubs. When a mother hunts, other pack members, called tenders, or wolf babysitters, guard and play with the cubs. Cubs are gently cared for by other pack members at places called rendezvous sites, where they explore their world, play, doze and wait for their parents to return. Pack members give cubs partially digested food, and they romp and play with them. Wolf parents and families are very indulgent with cubs. Cubs tweak adult ears, pull tails and bite; but they are cuddled, licked and loved.

From the earliest age, cubs vie with one another. They wrestle, have mock battles, stalk one another and play other games. These are important activities for building strength and agility. A cub's play also helps ascertain its future position, role and status in the pack. Cubs, too, establish a hierarchy among themselves. This is a shifting hierarchy—not permanent; their place in the pack will change many times. One of the first status tests is who eats first, and where, from the mother wolf. The back nipples have the most milk, so the little wolves struggle with one another for those nipples. They also compete for warmth and the mother's attention. Cubs are weaned by eight weeks. At that time, they continue to eat food regurgitated by other wolves and begin stalking bugs, mice and one another. Young wolves mouth the muzzles of older wolves to beg for food. The cubs' adult teeth start coming in when they are six months old, and they begin to hunt small things for themselves. Despite the love and care of the pack, cub mortality is high—only 50 percent of young ones survive their first year. Half succumb to disease, hunger and accidental death.

Young wolves have a lot to learn. In most packs, the alpha pair are everyone's parents, so life revolves around family politics and hunting. Young wolves must learn wolf etiquette and manners. They must observe the world around them and learn how to interact within the pack and with other animals, and how to hunt. They learn nuances of communication, not only by making sounds but also by using body language and eye contact and by relying on their senses.

Wolves play throughout their lives. Playing reinforces affection and bonds within the pack. The universal invitation to play is the bow; with the front legs flat on the ground and the rear end high in the air, the wolf utters a "woof" and demands attention. Once the invitation is accepted, activities like wolf tag, wrestling, mouthing, playing leap-frog, tug-of-war, and chasing feathers, rocks, pieces of wood and even other animals—like ravens or crows—ensue. Playtime is essential for wolves, as it is with all intelligent animals.

Wolves establish and patrol a large area of land—from twenty or so square miles to more than one thousand square miles in size—called their territory. In the wolf mind, all the prey animals, water, plants and the land itself within this territory is the domain of their own pack. They mark their territory with urine and feces. Wolf packs regularly walk their territorial boundaries and will fight to protect their lands from the intrusion of other wolf packs.

Alpha wolves mate for life, and their cubs stay with them. The hierarchy protects the pack. It offers everyone a place. Hierarchy determines feeding order and prevents quarrels from becoming fatal battles. The entire pack answers to the alpha pair. It is my observation that the alpha female generally controls the pack, and that the alpha male and female consider themselves equals. Alpha females are strict disciplinarians, and often the alpha male intercedes when her discipline gets too harsh. In my work with wolves, I have witnessed the way parents force their cubs to obey. For minor transgressions, the parent gently grasps the cub's muzzle in his or her mouth, forcing the cub down to the ground into a submissive position. For more serious transgressions, the alpha bites the cub on the muzzle or above the eye on the brow, then grasps the cub's muzzle and pushes the cub into submission. Sometimes cubs will endure several bites; at this point, the other parent usually intercedes and stops the discipline.

Wolves communicate through touching, vocalizing, body posture and scent-marking. Rank is established by ritualized aggression. A wolf stressing dominance will approach other wolves with raised tail, raised fur on the back and erect ears, and will stare at other wolves—directly into their eyes. In fights, the dominant wolf pins the adversary to the ground and growls in the other wolf's face. Submissive gestures include approaching a dominant wolf with the tail low, wagging the tail loosely, keeping the ears flat against the head and avoiding eye contact. In a fight, the submissive wolf lies on its back, with the tail curved to protect the belly and ears flat, and it makes a whining sound. These ritualized behaviors protect weaker wolves from being hurt in real fights and ensure order in the community.

When a real fight erupts, ritual posturing ends it. When a pack member challenges the existing order, wolves push each other to the ground, bare their fangs, snarl and make a tremendous uproar. The loser submits by exposing its belly and whining. Usually, no one is hurt. Sometimes if a wolf does not submit, the dominant wolf mauls it.

Lower-ranking wolves regularly show respect for dominant wolves. They have elaborate greetings: Subordinate wolves bow to their leaders, roll over on their backs, groom the alphas and lick their muzzles.

When wolves play, they make guttural, growling sounds. When cubs receive food, they get excited and squeak. Wolf sounds can be intimidating to the casual observer, but if one is fortunate enough to observe wild wolves, or to care for captive wolves, one learns to distinguish sounds, physical postures and other communications. Wolves are very expressive.

Fighting within a pack usually occurs only when food is involved—hence a pecking order is established and the higher in status eat first. When a pack member leaves the pack for an extended period of time and then returns, it must be readmitted to the group. If it is allowed to return, it has an omega rank and must reclimb the hierarchy ladder.

Wolf-pack leadership is determined by strength and decision making. Some observers could call this "reasoning"—who prepares the best hunting strategy, who provides the best for the pack, and so on. No rank is permanent: rank can change within a pack, and even the alpha rank can change.

When a young wolf leaves the pack to set out on its own and search for a mate to establish a new pack, the process is called *dispersal.* No one really knows what makes a wolf decide to leave its family. Wolf bonds are strong. Some ethologists speculate that omegas get fed up with their submissive roles and strike out alone to find better lives. Others speculate that some wolves are more independent-minded than others and make a decision to live separate from their parents. Perhaps it is an instinctive way to limit pack population and over-exploitation of game. Some 60 percent of wolves leave their packs by age two. Biologists have tracked wolves as far as 500 miles away from their original packs during dispersal. Lucky youngsters find mates and start their own packs. Unlucky ones fail in the search and die. Sometimes lone wolves are accepted into other packs, but this is a tricky business—a wolf risks its life when it seeks acceptance by a strange pack. The price of rejection is usually death.

Family Bonds and Communication

Usually, wolves find one mate and stay with that mate for life. In rare instances, wolves leave one mate for another. And sometimes an alpha male will have two alpha females: an alpha triad. When a mate dies, the bereaved one grieves, as does the entire pack. Sometimes the widowed alpha will find another mate. Wolves are affectionate and loving to each other. During the late-winter and early-spring mating season, this affection becomes even more obvious, as this is breeding time.

The alpha pair spends all of their time together, nuzzling, hugging, kissing and cuddling. When the female becomes pregnant, the male zealously provides for her needs—bringing extra food, becoming extra-vigilant. In the pack, even though the alpha male is usually bigger than the female, the female exercises a tremendous amount of control over the alpha male and the entire pack. The alpha female chooses the den site, prevents subordinate females from mating and rears her cubs for the first few weeks after birth until their introduction to the rest of the family.

The alpha male protects the pack and the breeding female and cubs. He prevents other males from mating, and he chases away intruders and initiates group howls. All pack members hunt, provide support for one another and care for cubs who leave the birthing den and enter wolf society.

During courtship time, the lead pair may keep separate from the rest of the pack and concentrate on each other. They cuddle, play and sleep together. They groom each other and make soft guttural utterances to each other—sounds of affection. The male can tell when the female is most receptive to mating advances by the scent of certain hormones and pheromones in her urine. When she enters ovulation, which is a period of five to seven days, she is ready to mate. That is the only time she will allow copulation with her partner. When not receptive, she will be moody and snap at her mate if he makes advances. After mating, the mother prepares her den. The pack waits with concern and anticipation for the arrival of new brothers and sisters. After about two months, the cubs are born and the entire pack is filled with joy. From the day they are born, cubs are loved, and they begin to learn the complicated ways of wolf society.

Communication is essential in the lives of social animals like wolves, and it is one of the most highly evolved and complex elements of wolf life. Evolution has shaped wolf senses to prepare them for life in a challenging and demanding world.

Wolves have excellent hearing. Their large, pointed ears are designed to detect even faint sounds—like mice or voles beneath the ground—and they can hear the howls of other wolves up to twelve miles away. Wolves can move their ears almost 180 degrees to discover the location of a sound, and they have a much broader range of hearing than humans do.

They hear all the same sounds that people can, but they can detect softer sounds and sounds in higher frequencies—up to 70,000 hertz (Hz). Humans cannot hear frequencies above 30,000 Hz. Wolves can hear mice walking in their underground nests. They can hear the soft steps of deer, the rustle of a rabbit hopping through fallen leaves. Wolf hearing is an amazing thing. Some scientists postulate that wolf ears are listening for sounds of danger even while the wolf sleeps. Wolves also use their ears in body-language communication.

In addition to hearing sounds of prey, of danger and of daily life, and listening to each other, wolf communication includes posturing, scent-marking and detecting scents, positioning of ears and tail, and vocalizations, which can be series of grunts, soft mutterings, howls, yips, growls, whines or woofs. Wolves rarely bark, and when they do, it is usually to warn of some approaching danger.

The most recognizable expression of wolf communication is the howl. All over the world, people associate the howling wolf with wilderness; wolf howls are considered by many to be the "Call of the Wild." But most people do not know why wolves howl.

Wolves howl for many reasons. They howl with the first light of the sun as part of their morning routine. Howls call the family together before hunting. Howls say hello and good-bye to pack members. Howls mourn the loss of a pack member. Howls let other wolves know where one territory begins and another ends. And sometimes, wolves howl just for the joy of being alive. Every wolf has his or her own distinctive voice and howl, like every human has a unique voice. Each pack member knows the voices of the others, as well as their individual scents. To hear wolves singing on a moonlit night or with the false dawn—what the ancient Greeks called "Wolflight"—is a powerful and moving experience.

Wolves use their sensitive noses to locate and track prey and to communicate with each other and other animals. Wolves scent-mark; they have special glands on the face, at the base of the tail, in the anus and on the paw pads. They identify secretions from these glands, in addition to feces and urine, to determine who left the marks. They can tell the age, sex, pack ranking and emotional state of the marking wolf from the scent.

Nature helped the wolf acquire such enhanced sensitivities through evolutionary development of an elongated snout containing billions of scent receptors. The reason wolves and other canines have wet noses is because moisture helps enhance the sense of smell. Like other animals, including dogs and cats, wolves have the Jacobson's organ. This is a lump at the back of the roof of the mouth. The organ is highly specialized in wolves; it detects scent and pheromones—it also lets the wolf know to stop eating when its stomach is full.

As territorial pack animals, wolves regularly patrol their territories and mark their boundaries. Strange wolves smell the biochemical messages. They can tell the age, sex and rank of the wolf who left the mark. If the scent has faded, the investigating wolf knows that the individual or pack has moved on. Wolves patrol and mark the same spots every day, so if the

scent has faded, other wolves know that the pack has left
the area.

Wolf Emotions and Body Language

Wolves are expressive and emotional creatures, and each wolf
has its own individual personality. There is as much individual
temperament among wolves as there is among human beings.
Some wolves are more gregarious than others. Some are mood-
ier and more aggressive than others. Wolves show their feelings
through body language. Body postures, ear and tail movements,
eye contact or avoidance, and accompanying vocalizations
clearly indicate wolf feelings.

Rules of Nature may be hard for humans to understand. To
some people, life in a wolf pack may seem harsh. But spend-
ing time with wolves and watching them through the seasons
makes one reconsider. Despite rigid pack hierarchy, every wolf
has a place in the family. Wolves defend each other. They are
emotionally bonded. They develop friendships with other animals—like ravens and crows. Wolves are sensitive and aware of
their surroundings. They take an interest in other animals—
and not just for hunting. I have seen young wolves cavort with
other young creatures—little fox kits, wandering coyote cubs,
even buffalo calves. These wolves are not the indiscriminate
killers of the European imagination.

When a wolf feels confident and secure, it raises its tail high
like a flag. When they want to play, they do the "play bow."
When they are fearful, or willing to submit to a dominant wolf,

they tuck their tails between their legs. When a wolf rolls over on its back, exposing its belly, it is demonstrating submission.

Growls, forward-pointing ears, and the tail sticking out straight and stiff show aggression. Wolves will sometimes stare and growl in aggression. When wolves are unsure about a situation; when they are not certain whether to be aggressive or they have mixed emotions, they will show mixed body language as well.

Wolf love, wolf aggression and wolf grief are powerful emotions, and wolves show them freely. Wolf grief is tragic to see. When a mate or pack member dies, wolves become sad. Once-playful, romping wolves become sullen. They mope. They lower their tails, draw their ears down and hang their heads. They cry, moan, whimper and shiver with grief. Sometimes they hide. Family groups will howl long, sad cries of heart-breaking sorrow and pain. They will not eat. Sometimes, when a mate dies, the widowed wolf will die of grief.

In Wolf Haven, a refuge for captive wolves in the Pacific Northwest, one female who had lost her mate was so sad that she would not eat or play. She lay down and waited to die. Wolf Haven had accepted shipment of what they were told was a.male wolf from Spokane, Washington. It was actually a wolf hybrid, which the staff realized after the animal arrived. But he looked like a wolf. The grieving female took an immediate interest in him and withdrew from her grief. The staff was thrilled—they feared she would grieve until she died. The female accepted the new "wolf," and together they built a new life.

People who hunt wolves are not ignorant about the ties
that bind packs together. One method they use for destruction
is to capture a young cub and tie it out as bait for family members. The terrified cub's cries bring the family to attempt a
rescue. The result is a slaughter of innocents.

I once cared for a wolf born with a defective liver. Just before his second birthday, the birth defect killed him. His family was devastated. His younger sister from a later litter went
into grief; crying, hiding and touching neither food nor water
for four days. His mother was restive the night he died. For
weeks after his death, his parents howled and moaned. I, too,
suffered a sense of tremendous loss. Wolves are not the only
animals that bond.

Sight is another sense that wolves use for communication
and survival. Some people comment on the ability of wolf eyes
to "glow in the dark." Wolves have a layer of cells behind the
retina called the *tapetum lucidum*. These cells help light reflect
from the retina and back outward, which helps the wolf see
better in the night. Wolf eyes have two types of receptor
cells—rods, which detect light intensity, and cones, which
detect color. Color detection is not as well developed in canines as in humans, but wolves can still see some color. Wolf
eyes are set on the front of the face, which helps them gauge
depth and locate their prey more effectively. Wolves have a
large sight range—a vision field of 270 degrees. Humans have
a field of vision of 100 degrees.

Evolutionary engineering crafted the wolf into a masterpiece of Nature: intelligent, sociable, a determined persistence

hunter and a master predator. Wolves were one of the most successful species on the planet for thousands of years. Their continued survival, despite human persecution and diminished numbers, is a testament to their intelligence and adaptability. But what is wolf life like? Examination of daily life is integral to understanding wolves and their world.

A Day in the Life of a Wolf

The wolf awakes before dawn. He breathes in the scent of fresh grass and pine trees and morning dew as he uncurls himself, shakes and stretches. He hears leaves rustling, he sighs and yawns as the rest of the pack awakens. His parents, brothers and sisters arise. They nuzzle one another, and stretch and yawn. In the light of the false dawn, his father, the alpha male, howls. One by one, other wolves yip and whine and join in the morning chorus. After the alpha male and his mate, the alpha female, begin the howl, the rest of the family joins in. As if on cue, the sun rises above fir-clad hills when the last wolf stops singing.

The wolves listen to the dawn cries of birds as they trot down to a small pool for their morning drink. After drinking, the smallest wolf, a female, her rump high in the air and her paws on the ground, offers an invitation for play and every one romps. Wolf hijinks ensue—a rough-and-tumble game of tag culminates in a group wrestling match.

As the sun climbs higher, the alpha pair head over to a cache from the previous day—the remains of a moose. They hear the croaks of ravens and the caws of magpies as they approach the

carcass. As they walk around a small bend, they spy a lone coyote chewing on a piece of crushed bone. Not much remains of
the old moose, but the big wolf will not tolerate intruders on
his prey. The birds scatter. The alpha male bristles with indig-
nation and makes an aggressive rush toward the forlorn and
frightened coyote. Coyote yips, tucks tail and runs. The big
male does not pursue the chase. He turns and tugs at the left-
over meat. His mate joins him. The rest of the family enters
the clearing. They politely wait until the parents are done eating. Then, one by one, they go and get pieces of the leftovers.

The young male grabs a remnant of leg bone and hunkers
down for a long chew, cracking the bones and sucking out the
marrow. As he chews, two ravens circle warily over his head.
They back off. One lands silently a few feet behind him. He
waddles up to the wolf's tail, takes it into his big, black beak
and gives it a tug. The wolf drops his bone and turns to snap
at the raven. The raven squawks, and laughs and flies away.
The wolf smiles and returns to his bone. This happens several
times; it is clearly a game both have played with each other
many times before.

The young wolf grows sleepy as the sun climbs high into
a noontime sky. The early rising, the play, the food and the
warm sunlight all combine to make him dozy. He walks away
from the feeding ground and into deep shade, walks in a small
circle, padding down leaves and grass, and lies down. He
sleeps. His parents embark on a walk around the pack's immediate territory. His father wants to make sure that the coyote
isn't lurking around.

The other wolves wisely take a relaxing siesta at midday.

When the young male awakens, he stretches and walks toward a stand of huckleberries. It's late summer, and the huckleberries are ripe and inviting. He nibbles on some plump, juicy ones. Suddenly, his ears perk up; he leans forward and puts his nose to the ground. He pounces up and then puts his paws down. He starts digging—he has heard a mouse and caught its scent. He digs quickly, but not quickly enough. The mouse has heard him coming and flees down a separate burrow and out behind the berry bushes. A wolf sister, attracted by the ruckus, trots over to see the cause of the excitement. She gobbles some berries and begins to tease her brother. They wrestle and roll.

After the tumble, both are thirsty, and they head back to the rocky pool for a late-afternoon drink. Squirrels chatter and throw pine cones at them as they walk. The wolves deliberately ignore the squirrels. They arrive at the pool and drink deeply. As they walk on the path away from the pool, they spy a family of skunks heading down the same path to the water. A mother, father and three little skunks shuffle toward them. The wolves look at each other, and then turn and high-tail it away from the skunk family. They know too well the consequences of an uninvited skunk encounter. The skunks proceed to the water with an air of confidence.

The two wolves make a circle and rejoin the wildlife path. They amble back to the sleeping place of the previous night. Their sister is already waiting for them there. Once again, an invitation to play is issued: The sister bows, and all three begin a romp. Their parents return from their daily travels about an

hour before sunset. All three young wolves trot out to greet
them and roll over on their backs in obeisance. With the arrival of twilight, the wolves sit on their haunches and watch
the setting sun. In appreciation of its beauty, the father howls
and the rest of the pack joins in. The crescent moon rises with
the indigo darkness and the stars shine bright in the heavens.
The wolves become sleepy. The alpha pair curl up beside each
other. The young ones sleep close together on the forest floor.
Another day has come and gone.

Dancing on the Razor's Edge

*M*an and wolf shared the earth for untold generations. At some point in time, human attitudes toward wolves started to change. The wolf, once honored as a companion and protector of the gods, respected for keen intelligence and survival skills, became the target of fear and hatred.

Some scholars attribute the change in attitude to the advent of settled agricultural lifestyles and the new perception of animals and even other people as property rather than as equals. Some scholars attribute changes in attitude to the ascension of Christianity in western Europe, but this is far too simplistic. Europeans had a strange, almost schizophrenic attitude toward wolves even before the conversion of Constantine to the Christian Mystery religion. The Romans, whose legendary founders, Romulus and Remus, were abandoned by humans and exposed in the wilderness, where they were rescued and suckled by a she-wolf, honored wolves. Yet, with the rise of empire, they routinely rounded wolves up to be slaughtered in the arena to the cheers and delight of the masses. Many species were driven to extinction to amuse the Roman *populi*.

Despite the use of captive wolves for sport and the bounties paid for wolf pelts, as long as human populations remained limited and the forests of Europe survived, the wolf survived. The advent of the Industrial Revolution and the expansion of human numbers and subsequent loss of natural habitat, coupled with the mass production of killing weapons like steel traps, repeating rifles and poisons, and the most massive human migrations in the history of the planet to the Western Hemisphere, all pushed wolves to the brink of extinction.

Civilized Europeans hunted wolves—some out of fear and for protection of their livestock. Some hunted for sport. Some killed for bounties. Some believed that all predators—wolf, bear, fox, coyote, wolverine, cougar, lion, tiger, eagle and hawk—should be destroyed to improve numbers of deer, elk and moose herds and other prey animals. Scientific observation and evidence demonstrates that this is a fallacy. Healthy herds have been molded for thousands of years by their predators, who have in turn been molded by the habits and behaviors of their prey. In the Western Hemisphere, large numbers of wolves flourished because of the thriving game herds. The most massive migrations in human history—those to the New World—stretched ecological balance to the breaking point and ushered in permanent changes in lands, peoples and ecologies. Sadly, many creatures did not survive the invasions.

By the end of the eighteenth century, wolves were essentially eradicated from the original thirteen states. As Euro-Americans crossed the Appalachians, they destroyed the forests, trapped and shot predators and shaped the land to their own design. After the American Revolution and the

destruction of the *Haudenosaunee,* the League of the Iroquois,
the only viable political and military obstacles to the Americans had been eliminated. American expansion escalated. With
the purchase of Louisiana from France, American control of
the West was secured. No one was certain of what was out in
the Louisiana territory, so in 1803, President Thomas Jefferson
sent a team of explorers led by Meriwether Lewis and William
Clark on a mission of paramount diplomatic, political, scientific and economic importance, to determine what was west of
the Mississippi.

During the expedition, Captain Clark wrote in his journals
about the numerous prairie wolves and their gentle nature.
He noted that they seemed like shepherds of the buffalo: "I
observe near all large gangues of Buffalow wolves and when
the buffalow move those animals follow, and feed on those
that are killed by accident or those that are too pore or fat to
keep up with the gangue . . . [the wolves] were fat and extremely gentle."

The mission of Jefferson's Corps of Discovery was successful. They traversed the Mississippi and Missouri rivers, seeking
the fabled water passage and the Great River of the West. They
established diplomatic contacts with the tribes. They described
vast landscapes of a rich and formidable territory. They wrote
about its creatures, plants, climates and water sources. With
the assistance of helpful tribes like the Mandan, Shoshone and
Nez Perce and the guidance of Sacajawea, they survived the
trek to the Pacific Ocean and back.

Through the journals of Lewis and Clark, images of a time

and place now lost forever were preserved—when America was a young and hopeful nation, seeking to make peace among and between the tribes; embracing the Louisiana land and its resources but not yet destroying them. The observations of the Corps of Discovery showed to future generations the powerful movement of the buffalo herds and the amazing ecosystems to which they belonged; an Eden where people and animals needed each other and had struck a life covenant together.

Americans were most interested in the Oregon country and California after the 1849 discovery of gold. They viewed the Great Plains and the Rocky Mountains as uninhabitable until gold and silver were discovered there as well. The American Civil War slowed down westward expansion for a while, but the flood of Euro-Americans resumed after the war. By 1900, the Americans had driven wolves to the edge of extinction in lands west of the Mississippi. The tribes, too, were pushed to the edge of oblivion. The wolves were dying. The buffalo were gone. The prairie was destroyed—rain did not follow the plow. More and more sod-busting farmers established themselves in the plains, and by the 1930s, they had turned the region into a raging, blustery desert. Some say the Dust Bowl and the "Dirty '30s," were divine retribution for American abuse of the land and its denizens, human and nonhuman.

At the urging of ranchers and farmers, the United States Government set bounties on wolves and other predators; the grizzly and black bear, the cougar, the lynx, the fox, the coyote. Americans shot the wolves. They poisoned wolves. They burned them alive. They hunted them and found their dens and butchered their young ones. They scoured the deserts of the Southwest and killed the Mexican *lobos*. They invaded the mountains and killed the wolves there. They destroyed the buffalo herds and all the life they supported, including Lewis's "extremely gentle" buffalo wolves. Concurrently, the federal government subsidized expansion of the railroads, federal laws subsidized corporate mining ventures and ranchers took up leases on public lands for running their cattle.

"The invaders treated every living thing in the same way—they hunted us. They wanted our land so they tried to exterminate us," one modern Cheyenne Dog Soldier explained. "The buffalo, the wolf, the land, the water. They wanted it all. So they killed everything that they feared. . . . What they did to the wolves was what they were doing to us, too. As it goes with our brother the wolf, so, too, it goes with us."

No one knows exactly how many wolves were killed between 1860 and 1900, but some sources estimate the number at one million. Other sources say two million. Despite all attempts to exterminate them, a few packs survived in the Lower Forty-Eight. Canadian and Alaskan packs fared better due to their isolation—at least until the 1960s, when oil was discovered in Alaska.

As legendary leaders arose among the tribes in an attempt to defend lands and people—Tashunka Witco (Enchanted Horse, aka Crazy Horse), Sitting Bull, Morning Star, Little Wolf, Chief Joseph, Cochise, Geronimo, Captain Jack and many others, so did legendary wolves emerge as symbols of wild resistance. Two famous Montana wolves jump from the book of legends. Ghost Wolf and Snowdrift were outlaw wolves, as famous and notorious as Billy the Kid, Jesse James, Butch and Sundance or Belle Starr. Reporters called these wolves "outlaws." The state of Montana and the federal government offered special bounties for them. From 1915 to 1930, these amazing wolves seem to have declared war on ranchers and their livestock.

Old Montanans still tell legends of the wolf outlaws. They say that Ghost Wolf was first seen in the Judith Basin country of Montana around 1915. Ghost's range was about a million acres, stretching from the Highwood Mountains to the Little Belt Range. Around 1920, the Ghost "turned outlaw," according to the old ranchers. He started bringing down cattle, horses, sheep, goats. Ghost developed a nationally notorious reputation when the Associated Press ran accounts of his war on ranchers in the 1920s. Cattlemen offered a reward for the Ghost Wolf and distributed "Wanted Dead or Alive" posters throughout the Rocky Mountain West. They offered a reward of $400 for the Ghost Wolf. Men formed posses to "bring the wolf to justice."

Ghost Wolf is credited with killing more than 2,000 head of livestock in the 1920s. How much was the work of the Ghost and how much was the work of dog packs—and how much was the exaggeration of traumatized ranchers—is unclear. But men devoted their intelligence and the power of twentieth-century technology to their determination to kill the Ghost Wolf.

From 1920 to 1930, wolf-killers set out traps and poison,

determined to destroy him. They hunted him with airplanes.
They chased him with cars. They pursued him on horseback,
on foot, through winter drifts with snowshoes. After a decade
of outwitting his enemies, Ghost Wolf was brought to his
doom by two canids and a hominid—a rancher named Al
Close, a terrier named Mike and a sheep dog named Nick.
The trio tracked Ghost Wolf in May of 1930, and Close
gunned him down.

The great wolf-outlaw Snowdrift also rose to notoriety in
the 1920s. He ranged from the Judith Basin to the Little Belt
Mountains and into the Bear Paw Mountains. He had suffered
the loss of one toe from his left paw to the cruel jaws of a trap,
so his tracks were distinctive. Like the Ghost Wolf, Snowdrift
had fair fur. He is accused of killing some 1,500 cattle, and
ranchers alleged that he cost them over $30,000 in lost stock.
Federal wolf-killers Don Stevens and Stacy Eckert snared Snowdrift in a leg-trap in 1923. Somehow, the courageous desperado
wrenched the trap loose from the ground. The government
men chased him, with the trap on his front paw, for four long
days before they finally cornered and shot the noble Snowdrift.

The State of Montana paid $360,000 in wolf bounties for
more than 80,000 wolves between 1884 and 1933. Finally, in
1933, Montana removed the bounty provision from their state
books, because there had been no wolves delivered to collect
the $15-per-head reward for many years. There just weren't
many wolves left to kill in Montana.

Ghost Wolf and Snowdrift were Montana wolves. Other
famous outlaws include the Sycan Wolf of Oregon, the Custer

Wolf and Pine Ridge Wolf of South Dakota, the Pryor Wolf of Montana's Crow Indians, and Old Whitey from Colorado.

Many of the American West's "outlaw wolves," were white wolves. Medicine people of the Nez Perce, Lakota, Cheyenne and Crow people say that a white wolf, like a white buffalo, is a sacred entity. "Well, all life is sacred, as you know," one Nez Perce explained. "But the Creator sends us down special ones to remind us of important things. These white wolves, they are a message from God. They remind us that we better take care of things. It is wrong to ignore their messages."

Many Native Americans still honor old ways and respect the old messengers. Indian tribes have played key roles in wolf survival and the reintroduction of wolves into their ancient territories.

By the 1960s, wolves were almost gone from the Lower Forty-Eight. A few red wolves, smaller cousins of the gray wolf, survived in the Southeast. There were wolves in Alaska and Canada, but they were increasingly threatened by human encroachment, damage to caribou calving grounds and energy-resource development. Biologists with the group Defenders of Wildlife, a Nature advocacy group, estimate that only 60,000 wolves remained in North America by the late 1960s, and most of those were in Alaska. By 1973, habitat destruction by human development, bounty programs and federal trappers had eliminated wolves from every Lower Forty-Eight state except Minnesota, where there were still about 400 wolves. It seemed like wolves were doomed.

But in the 1950s and 1960s, changes were sweeping the

hearts and minds of many Americans. American identity has
always been shaped by Nature and the land. Whether it was
fear of Nature and domination of the land, as in the Puritan
days; or exploitation and domination of the land, its resources
and its peoples as in the days of Manifest Destiny; or destruction of land and habitat in the opening decades of the twentieth century, Nature is integral to the unique identity of
America as a nation. Philosophical seeds grew in the popular
mind, planted by writers like Herman Melville in his masterpiece about God, Nature, human obsession and the great
white whale, *Moby-Dick*; John J. Audubon and his interest in
birds; the American Transcendentalists Emerson and Thoreau;
and even Edgar Allan Poe. Thoughts of Sacred Nature combined with an awakening of the American consciousness
demonstrated by writers like Aldo Leopold, Lois Crisler and
Rachel Carson to make Americans reassess their relationship
with the land, her creatures and even other human beings—
like Native Americans and Black Americans. The G.I. Bill produced more and better-educated Americans than ever before.
The Beat movement led to generations of questioning. Their
children, the hippies, continued the quest. Civil rights and
economic-parity movements, including the Black and American Indian Movement and the Great Society, focused attention
on many inequities in the American system. The turbulent
Sixties opened the doors to many vast changes in American
society.

People demanded changes in federal attitudes and regulations involving the natural world. In 1963, Aldo Leopold's son,

A. Starker Leopold, chaired a national panel that concluded that national parks should protect "primitive America." In 1973, the new federal Endangered Species Act reflected this national awakening. It outlawed the injury or killing of any animal belonging to a species on the brink of extinction. It was the beginning of the long road to wolf recovery.

The Endangered Species Act was signed into law by President Richard Nixon. The law mandated that the U.S. Fish and Wildlife Service (USFWS) prepare recovery plans for threatened and endangered species. The gray wolf was the first species listed as endangered under the new law. American citizens demanded wolf survival.

Not everyone embraced protection of endangered species—especially predators like wolves and grizzly bears. Many ranchers and developers voiced concerns. Land developers lobbied against any federal or state controls that would interfere in acquisition of land for profit. Ranchers worried that wolves would decimate their herds. People were terrified that wolves would endanger their pets and children. The fear of wolves is deeply ingrained in many people, and extensive community and individual education is essential to successful wolf recovery. The majority of Americans demand wolf recovery, but the majority of Americans live in places where there are no wolves. The USFWS faced and continues to face major obstacles in destroying misconceptions about wolves and overcoming prejudice against them. The group holds public hearings and public-education workshops on an ongoing basis about wolf reintroduction and living with predators.

Many ranchers feel squeezed between fluctuations in de-

mand for beef, federal wildlife regulations and trying to make
ends meet to support their families. As demand for beef has
decreased, more and more ranchers face hard decisions about
their livelihoods. Some have turned to the tourism and service
economies and become outfitters, leading trophy hunts for
game. Many ranchers-turned-outfitters embrace the old fallacy
that wolves take the biggest and strongest deer, elk or moose.
Once again, this places rancher and predator in direct compe-
tition, at least in the rancher's imagination. In Catron County
in the Gila country of New Mexico, one rancher makes tremendous profits guiding trophy hunts for elk. His concern
about reintroduction of the Mexican wolf to its old homeland
is fear of losing profit. He publicly worries that wolves will
take the prime game that his trophy-hunters want to kill, and
that he will no longer make easy money leading hunts on his
leased federal grazing lands.

Another Gila country rancher hates both wolves and their
prey. In the summer of 2000, he killed more than 150 doe elk
and their calves because they ate grass on his federal leasehold-
ing. When asked by USFWS officers why he had killed them,
he said he didn't want them eating the food for his cattle and
he didn't want the reintroduced Mexican wolves to have food.

The livestock industry is the most active opponent of wolf
recovery. Ranchers in Wyoming and Montana call wolves
"cow-killers" and "breeding machines" because wolves can pro-
duce cubs yearly as long as they have good food sources. Before implementation of the Endangered Species Act and wolf
reintroduction, these same ranchers hated coyotes, eagles and
cougars and blamed them for livestock losses. Federal wildlife

studies conducted in Minnesota indicate that wolves prefer native prey—deer, elk, moose, rabbit or mice—to domesticated stock and rarely kill livestock—a fraction of one percent of total livestock-loss numbers. Since the reintroduction of wolves into the Yellowstone country in 1995, wolf packs have rarely clashed with ranching interests and depredation by wolves has been low. Defenders of Wildlife has established a compensation fund that pays ranchers market value for livestock losses due to wolf depredation. Federal agents destroy wolves that persist in killing livestock.

Wolves have been restored in areas of the Northern Rockies, and the Mogollon/Gila country of the Great Southwest. In Alaska, wolves were not listed as endangered, so state regulations governed them. Reintroduction is under consideration in the Northeast. In Maine and Vermont, there have been reports of wolf sightings but no proof of permanent breeding populations. In the Upper Great Lakes region, Minnesota has a thriving wolf population. The wolves of Isle Royale National Park on Lake Superior are international celebrities and have been studied intensively. Wolves also have reappeared in Michigan. By the early 1960s, most wolves had been eliminated from the region, except in Minnesota. But wolves naturally recolonized their old homeland by walking back as their numbers grew.

Wolves were eliminated from the Pacific Northwest in the 1930s, but in recent years, wolves have been moving into Washington State from British Columbia. Wolves have been moving into eastern Oregon and eastern Washington as Idaho wolves recover and expand their ranges.

A special wolf survives in the swamps, marshes and pine
forests of the Southeastern United States. This is the diminutive red wolf, *Canis rufus*. This species is distinct from the gray
wolf, *Canis lupus*. Some paleo-geneticists speculate that the red
wolf is the ancient ancestor of the gray wolf. Citing new devel-
opments in DNA studies, they maintain that the red wolf
evolved in North America and dispersed globally. Many generations later, their descendants developed into a separate species,
the gray wolf, and those wolves walked back to the Western
Hemisphere across the Bering Land Bridge.

The red wolf is a small wolf, with reddish-brown markings.
When the British first settled Roanoke, the wolves they found
there were probably red wolves. This little wolf once ranged
throughout the Southeast and as far west as Texas, but they
were almost extinct by the 1960s. By the 1980s, the red wolf
was extinct in the wild, and only a few pairs survived in captive breeding facilities.

Under the guidelines of the Endangered Species Act, the
USFWS teamed up with the Point Defiance Zoo and Aquar-
ium in Tacoma, Washington, to undertake ensuring the survival of the red wolf. Wolf-recovery team members removed the
last survivors from the South. Removing a species from the wild
to establish a breeding program is a desperate measure, and not
something done lightly. It is only done when all other efforts
to preserve a species in its natural range have failed. Destruction of habitat and destruction of species go hand in hand,
and it is best to protect and conserve entire ecological systems.

By 1984, captive red wolves numbered sixty-three and their

population was growing under the federal Red Wolf Species Recovery and Survival Plan. In 1987, USFWS released the first wolves at the Alligator River National Wildlife Refuge in the Tidewater country of North Carolina. Today, there are about one hundred red wolves living in North Carolina, and all but two have been born in the wild. Another 170 reside in captivity. In the spring of 2002, two more cubs were born in the Alligator River wolf compound. By 2003, three new cubs were thriving under the care of a wild wolf mother. The red wolf is far from restored, but these small steps demonstrate the wolf's will to survive with a little human cooperation.

Currently, wolves are listed as endangered throughout the continental United States, except for Minnesota. Minnesota counts between 1,750 and 2,000 wolves, and the number is growing. Two areas in the West are especially interesting in relation to the rebirth of the wolf. These are the northern Rocky Mountains and the Gila Wilderness, where Aldo Leopold had his epiphany.

Wolves in the Northern Rockies

In the northern Rockies, around the Glacier Park area of northwestern Montana, the balance of nature has not been as damaged as the rest of the Lower Forty-Eight. The region is the interface of the United States-Canada border and the meeting of two national parks, Glacier on the American side and Waterton Lakes on the Canadian side. Because of this area's isolation and protected status, few humans live here. This is the

domain of wolf, cougar, bear, wolverine, pine marten and
lynx. Unlike other places in North America, nonhuman predators rule here. Biologists call an area along the North Fork of
the Flathead River, near Polebridge, Montana, "America's
Wildest Valley." It is a complex and complete ecosystem, re-
plete with moose, deer, elk and a wide variety of vegetations
and elevations. Human encroachment has not killed the
systems. Too often, islands of forest appear to be wild refuges,
yet in reality are merely remnants of a doomed ecosystem,
surrounded by human cities, highways and pollution, dying
a slow death. But in northwestern Montana, the link to wilderness is secure. Wolf and bear have not changed their ways to
accommodate humans. "Other places where there are predators tend to micromanage and modify predator behavior,"
Wildlife Conservation Society researcher John L. Weaver
explains. "But that is diminishment of wild behavior. Here,
animals can be what they are—truly wild."

Wolves from the Canadian side of the border have been
walking into the United States and recolonizing northwestern
Montana since the 1980s. The USFWS estimated that there
are now five packs in the region, consisting of some sixty-five
wolves. This is a healthy and thriving system.

Farther south, in Yellowstone National Park and central
Idaho, occasional wolf sightings were reported in the 1980s—
a lone wolf here or there—but there was no documented evidence of breeding pairs or families. Except for the Polebridge
region, federal trappers and bounty hunters effectively extir-
pated wolves from the American Rockies in the 1930s. In 1926,

the last wolves in Yellowstone, America's first national park, were killed as part of the federal predator extermination program. Back in those days, national parks were not looked upon as sanctuaries for all life—and especially not for predators. Aldo Leopold advocated for survival of the Yellowstone wolves in 1944, when he wrote, "Why in the necessary process of extirpating wolves from the livestock ranges of Wyoming and Montana, were not some of the uninjured animals used to restock the Yellowstone?" His pleas for wolf conservation were ignored for many years.

Eventually, as a consequence of public demand and the Endangered Species Act, federal wildlife officials developed wolf-recovery and -reintroduction plans. In May of 1994, USFWS presented its Final Environmental Impact Statement (FEIS), *The Reintroduction of Wolves to Yellowstone National Park and Central Idaho.* After letters of support by tens of thousands of American citizens and a series of public hearings, the reintroduction was approved. Wolves from Alberta, Canada, were the emissaries heralding the return of their species to the Yellowstone country.

Despite overwhelming support by Americans for the return of the wolf, some special-interest groups were determined to block it. Members of the American Farm Bureau Federation, whose affiliates in Wyoming, Montana and Idaho are descendants of the very pioneers whose invasion of the West has been orchestrated, supported and subsidized by the federal government from the days of Lewis and Clark through today, filed suit in federal district court to block reintroduction. For a century, federal planning and public subsidies supported ranch survival in the West. Yet when the same American public that had supported ranch development demanded that ranchers share the land with others, the ranchers resisted.

At a public hearing near Cody, Wyoming, in 1992, packed by anti-wolf people, U.S. Fish and Wildlife man and Wolf Recovery Coordinator Ed Bangs announced, "You all ought to be dad-gum happy it's not a vote. . . . We get boxes of mail every day from people who want the wolf back." The will of the people demanded that ranchers learn to live in balance with wolves, and some did not like it. The Mountain States Legal Foundation supported them in the suit. They sued the Department of the Interior. What followed was a legal roller-coaster. On January 3, 1995, their request for an injunction was denied by Judge William Downes of the Federal District Court in Cheyenne; this allowed reintroduction efforts to commence while the case proceeded. A few days later, with USFWS trucks loaded with wolves literally at the gates of Yellowstone Park, the Farm Bureau received an administrative stay, temporarily delaying return of the wolves. On January 12, the district court refused the Farm Bureau's request and allowed release of the wolves into acclimation pens in Yellowstone and into the mountains of central Idaho.

Something truly bizarre in the annals of American jurisprudence then occurred. On December 12, 1997, Judge Downes issued a ruling that the reintroduction had been illegal and that wolves should be removed from the Yellowstone and central Idaho ecosystems because, since a few wolves survived in

Idaho before the federal wolf reintroduction, wolves would lose protection under the federal special experimental, nonessential designation, and this would then make the reintroduction illegal under Downes's interpretation of the Endangered Species Act. As a result, one family of wolves from the Yellowstone country was taken in as brothers by the Nez Perce of Idaho, whose own ancestors had been hunted down by the Americans and their military in 1877, when they tried to escape the Americans and flee to Canada.

Legal wrangling continues. But wolves remain in the region, and today there are several packs, numbering some ninety individuals, in the Yellowstone region. There have been a few livestock depredations by wolves, and the Bailey Wildlife Foundation Wolf Compensation Trust of the Defenders of Wildlife has compensated ranchers for the rare occurrences. There have been several incidents of criminals killing wolves inside and outside the park. Some of these wolf-killers have used excuses like, "I thought it was a coyote," or "The wolf was after my dog," as defenses. These cases were investigated and the culprits tried and convicted. Ranchers and wildlife officials cooperate to remove or kill problem wolves who repeatedly attack and kill livestock. Not all ranchers oppose reintroduction. Some work very hard to reestablish a balance between predator conservation and sustainable livestock futures.

Many ranchers feel besieged. American dietary habits have changed, and interest in the beef industry has dropped. Small family operations are squeezed by huge corporate factory farms and ranching operations. Every year, it becomes harder for

small farmers and ranchers to support their operations or
break even. States like Montana, Idaho and Wyoming are still
agricultural states, and people want to leave family legacies to
their children. But the economic squeeze is a vise that tightens
year by year. To many ranchers, federal reintroduction of the
wolf felt like one more attack.

"It's like this to . . . ranchers and farmers. The real issue is
economics, not wolves. People feel that their lives are out of
control," Wolf Recovery head Ed Bangs explains. "They have
issues with the federal government and things like the Endangered Species Act. Wolves become symbols of these issues. . . .
In the fourteen years I have worked with wolves in Montana,
it seems like once people settle down and get beyond symbols
and postures, and the wolf becomes just another animal, people
begin to accept things. Look, people and wolves lived together
for thousands and thousands of years. It seems only when
people started raising livestock did the wolf become hated."

Bangs says that human attitudes, conflicts and politics
would promote lively debates about successful wolf recovery in
the Northern Rockies. "Small ranchers can't make a living just
ranching anymore because of market changes, and interest
rates and global shifts. So a lot of wealthy people and absentee
landlords have moved into Montana and Wyoming," Bangs
explains. "Different people moving into the region have
brought different attitudes towards wolves and other predators, so the discussions will continue."

One ranch woman, whose family was forced to give up
ranching due to market changes and corporate pressures, ex-

plained her feelings, "At first, I blamed the animals and the Endangered Species Act and federal interference. Our family is like so many others," the Hardin, Montana, resident said. "But I started thinking about it. The wolves, the cougars, the coyote, the deer, the rancher and the farmer; we are all under the same pressures. Those animals need someplace to go. They just want to live. And too much development and too many people moving in—it has put the squeeze on them [the animals], too. We can't blame the wolf—it's a human problem."

Many people forget that the land, the animals and the tribes belonged together long before the arrivals of the Europeans, who then imposed horrific changes on the land and its inhabitants. But the Wheel of Fortune has turned, spun by public demand in a democratic nation, and that demand has forced major changes in federal policy about land and wildlife management.

Euro-Americans are beginning to understand concepts of natural systems—for instance, that wolves, as predators, are essential members of the greater ecosystem. Before American domination of the land, the wolf was the primary predator of elk, bison and moose in the Yellowstone country; indeed, in most of the West. Without the wolves, the herds and the land suffered. Coyote populations expanded and became overabundant—filling in the empty wolf niche. But the little coyote is not a killer of big game. Coyote numbers dropped with wolf reintroduction, allowing fox numbers to grow. Wolves are a balancer—they cull bison and elk herds. As a result, the entire Yellowstone ecosystem is now flourishing. Reduction in elk and bison allowed regeneration of aspen and willow trees—too many deer and bison resulted in overgrazing. Even small birds benefit from the return of the wolf—many of them eat from the leftovers at kill sites.

The wolf offers benefits to those ranching families who are hard pressed to stay on the land. Rebirth of the wolf brings millions of new tourist dollars to Montana. People flock to the region to be close to wolves. The thrill of hearing wolfsong, even the mere hope of it, is enough to bring people to the area. Sine the return of the wolf to Yellowstone in 1995, the region has seen a boost of $10 million. Federal revenue projects indicate that as wolf reintroduction proceeds, additional revenues of $25 million every year will pour into the region. Ranching families determined to hold on to their homes can exploit this situation and lead wolf-study tours or establish dude ranches or boarding homes for visitors.

Visitors to Yellowstone Park consistently mention that the wolf is the main animal they come to see. In gateway towns like Red Lodge and Cooke City, Montana, tourist numbers have skyrocketed since 1995. An interesting aspect of this new wolf tourism is that visitors do not just travel in summer— they come to visit wolf country all year long. In a 2001 survey of Red Lodge merchants, 75 percent said that they believed interest in wolves brought in more tourists and more money.

By December of 2002, the Northern Rocky Mountain Wolf Recovery Project had achieved its goals. By the end of the month, federal estimates counted between 650 and 700 wolves in about forty-one breeding pairs throughout Montana.

According to Ed Bangs, this was the third year that northern Rocky Mountain wolf populations had thirty or more breeding pairs—indicating that wolf numbers had reached federal numerical and distributional recovery goals. The states of Montana, Idaho and Wyoming have proposals in place for wolf management plans, and the federal government will propose delisting of wolves as endangered species once the plans are approved.

Under the Endangered Species Act (ESA), federal protection is extended to every species facing extinction. In cases like those of the gray wolf, the red wolf and the California condor, tremendous effort, energy and funding are expended by federal and state wildlife people; private rehabilitation and Nature centers; zoos; ethologists; veterinarians and volunteers to ensure species survival. Under ESA guidelines, restored populations' survival is to be guaranteed by the states once an animal is removed from the endangered list. In the case of the northern Rocky Mountain region, wolf reintroduction seems to have been successful. The return of the wolf to the Gila country in the Great Southwest has not been as happy a tale.

Mexican Wolves of the Mogollon

Unlike their northern relatives, the Southwest's Mexican gray wolves face a far more dangerous and uncertain future. Hunted to virtual extinction in the wild from the 1800s through the 1960s, only about 200 Mexican wolves are left in the world, and most of them are in captive breeding and education programs. If not for these programs, Mexican wolves

would no longer exist. These beautiful creatures once ranged
from northern Mexico and western Texas into the Colorado
plateau and the Gila wilderness, where the Mogollon Rim
rises, dividing the Sonoran desert into its upper and lower
regions. This is the sacred homeland of the Hopi, Zuni and
Apache—a land of scattered mesas, mountain uplifts and
cedar-clad hills, home to the Storm Gods of the Mogollon,
whose clouds rise above the heat of summer and deliver the
land from its tormented thirst with blessed rain. A wild, sun-
drenched land of hills, plateaus and deep arroyos, this was
the place where Aldo Leopold received his enlightenment
while he hunted the Mexican wolf.

Years later, on March 28, 1998, the federal Wolf Recovery
Program released eleven Mexican wolves into the Apache
National Forest. Aldo Leopold's great-granddaughter, Patricia
Stevenson, carried one of them and released it home. Two
more wolves were released later that year. Twenty-one wolves
were returned home in 1999. Of the thirty-four wolves released, five have been deliberately shot by anti-wolf activists,
one has disappeared, five were recaptured and returned to captivity to save them, and two have been hit by cars, including
a female yearling, who died on Highway 89, northeast of
Flagstaff, Arizona. Mogollon wolves have not recovered as well
as their northern relatives. The federal goal was establishment
of a population of 100 wolves by 2003. It was not met. Resistance by a very few human opponents in the remote Mogollon
region is the primary obstacle to wolf recovery. The problem is
not fear of wolves, but human greed.

"The problem is not whether the wolves can live with human beings; the problem is whether the human beings will live with wolves," explains wolf specialist Judy Loeven of Wolf Haven International in Tenino, Washington. "In the case of wolf-recovery attempts in Alpine, Arizona, and the Gila country, there are plenty of game, plenty of land and plenty of space. Wolves are willing to share, but are the people willing to share space for wolves? That is the question."

Wolf Haven played a key role in reintroduction of Mexican wolves. Many of the Mogollon wolves were reared at Wolf Haven. Wolf Haven is one of five wolf centers in the United States. As part of the federal wolf recovery program, the center has raised Mexican wolves and prepared them for reintroduction into the wild. It is only one of three pre-release facilities—a last stop for wolves before they return to wilderness.

On March 26, 1998, the New Mexico Cattle Growers Association, the New Mexico Public Lands Council and the Catron County Farm and Livestock Bureau filed suit against the Department of the Interior and the U.S. Fish and Wildlife Service in an attempt to block wolf restoration to the Gila country. As plaintiffs, they alleged that:

- Federal agencies acted illegally when they reintroduced wolves, because Mexican gray wolves already inhabited parts of Arizona and New Mexico
- They would suffer irreparable harm because wolves would prey on livestock, wolves would invade private lands, uses of private lands would be restricted and the Service may take or condemn private property for the wolves

- Released Mexican wolves are not genetically pure, but are a dog or coyote mix
- The Service's Environmental Impact Statement was inadequate
- The Service violated the Endangered Species Act

Wolf advocates viewed the suit as spurious, and the courts ruled against the plaintiffs. The American public supports the return of the Mexican wolf, but a few people in the Gila country have their own reasons for resisting the popular will and breaking wildlife laws.

David Parsons, former head of the Mexican Wolf Recovery program, explains, "There is plenty of food for the wolves in the Gila country. The question is, do a few ranching families want to share the land with the wolves? The people who have killed five of the wolves obviously don't want to share, even though the American people demand wolf recovery."

At a February 2000 anti-wolf rally in Glenwood, deep in the Gila wilderness, several hundred vocal opponents of wolf recovery—most of them people from outside the state of New Mexico—convened to howl against wolf recovery. Local politicians surveyed the crowd. In discussions of their anti-wolf views, many resuscitated the old and discredited stereotypes of wolves, choosing to ignore the interwoven relationship between prey and predator. Many voiced concern for their cattle or pet dogs and cats. One man was certain that a wolf would eat his children. Some citizens insisted that there wasn't enough food for wolves in the Gila country. Ranchers who supplement their ranching income by leading trophy hunts on federal and state lands feared that wolves would take the best bucks and interfere with their hefty hunting profits.

With the decline of public interest in beef, and in a region where federal subsidies barely support ranchers and their families—who want to stay on lands that their ancestors took from the tribes—many Gila folks opt for work as guides for trophy hunters in order to make decent money. Under an unusual New Mexico policy, landholders need only sign up for a state land permit to be able to shoot as many deer or elk as they desire. This policy allows ranchers to sign up for permits and sell them to trophy hunters. The outfitter pockets the money and makes about $3,500 per bull elk.

"This is one of the real issues with ranchers opposing wolf reintroduction," USFWS officer Tom Bauer explained. "They are making money with the permit-and-trophy scheme, and they worry that wolf recovery will interfere with that money. The argument that there is not enough game to support wolves is not true, and the Baca situation clearly illustrates that."

Misunderstandings about wolves and game persist. "What these people don't understand is that wolves don't take the trophy elk," Wolf Haven Communications Director Julie Palmquist says. "Wolves take the sick, the maimed, the dying. Trophy hunters don't want those—they want the big bucks with the big racks."

Today there are fewer than thirty Mexican wolves roaming the Gila country, a small and controversial beginning. These wolves face an uncertain future. In field interviews with Gila country residents, many people said they did not have issues

with the wolves, but hated the federal government. Others
said they wanted the wolves back but were afraid to make their
support public, fearing retribution from the vocal and powerful few who do not want wolves back in the wilderness. Much
more communication, understanding and public education is
needed to insure the safety and survival of the Mexican wolf.

Indigenous Peoples and Wolf Recovery

Many indigenous peoples throughout the world support wolf
survival. The experience of too many tribal peoples in the past
five hundred years has sad parallels to European treatment of
wolves and other creatures. Among the North American tribes,
many people in the Yukon and Alaska still depend on the mi-
gration of caribou and the complicated ecological systems in
which they live. The Ojibway, Seneca, Mohawk, Oneida,
Onondaga, Tuscarora, Cherokee, Comanche and many others
support efforts at wolf recovery. Many tribes do not want
people to be allowed to hunt wolves for trophies or "sport"
ever again. Many tribes have clans that claim descent from
spirit entities of Wolf, Raven, Eagle or Bear. People remember
their own suffering and the decimation of the Great Plains
bison and the systems these animals supported. They remember their own suffering from strange diseases—smallpox,
measles, chicken pox—illnesses that destroyed entire villages
long before people even saw Europeans. They remember the
wars over land; forced relocation and loss of traditional ways.
They remember hunger and subjugation. They understand

that Americans ignore treaties; they have experienced the whims of Congress and the seesaw politics of the Indian Bureau and the Bureau of Indian Affairs. Tribal people relate to the wolf for a great many reasons. One tribe in particular is involved in a unique relationship with both wolves and the federal government. They offered sanctuary to wolves when federal courts and judicial policies betrayed one pack. That tribe is the Nez Perce; their name for themselves is *Nimipu.*

The Nez Perce homeland traditionally stretched from the Wallowa and Blue Mountains of Oregon to the Palouse hills and into the upper reaches of the Clearwater River and its tributaries in what is now called Idaho. One of their great gifts to the world was the Palouse Horse, termed "Appaloosa," by the newcomers. For centuries, these people lived quiet lives of fishing, hunting, gathering plants and camus roots, trading with other tribes and making seasonal hunts into the Buffalo Country of Montana and Wyoming, mounted on their spotted ponies. In 1805, when the American Corps of Discovery stumbled out of the Bitterroot Mountains, dazed and starving, the Nez Perce took care of them. They fed them, made them well and guided them to the Columbia River, which took them west to the ocean. The Nez Perce liked Lewis and Clark and became allies of the United States.

For fifty years they lived as friends with the New People, but tensions escalated as more and more Americans came to the Oregon country. The newcomers wanted land. In the mountains, they found silver and gold. They did not honor their commitments to their Indian allies. They wanted everything.

From 1855 to 1877, the Americans forced the Nez Perce to
give up the use of 95 percent of their traditional homeland—
over 13 million acres, and confine themselves to a small piece
of land near Lapwai, Idaho. American politicians and military
officers insisted that the Nez Perce move their families, their
horses and their homes in the midst of the spring flood season. The young men of the Nez Perce clashed with obnox-
ious miners and missionaries. Finally, in 1877, a year after the
Cheyenne, Arapahoe and Lakota humiliated the Americans
on the battlefield at Little Big Horn in the centennial year of
America's independence, several Nez Perce decided that the
only choice they had for survival was to flee from their beloved
homeland north to Canada. Under leaders Joseph (*In-mut-
too-yah-lat-kat,* Thunder Over the Land from the Water) and
Looking Glass and other brave people, they fled. But a Nez
Perce exodus wasn't enough for the Americans. They sent their
armies chasing after the refugees.

Greatly outnumbered by the American soldiers and leading
bands of old people, children and women, Nez Perce warriors,
determined to defend their families, defeated the U.S. Army in
many battles. The Nez Perce fled through Lolo Pass into the
Yellowstone country. They travelled through the Yellowstone
and tried to get to Canada. Finally, with his group outnumbered, outgunned and facing cannon and severe weather,
Joseph pled for the survival of his people when he pledged, "I
will fight no more. Forever," just a few miles south of sanctuary in Canada. Some Nez Perce made it across the border.
Those who surrendered faced forced relocation to Florida and
Oklahoma.

Joseph never stopped lobbying for the Nez Perce to be allowed to return home. In 1895, support from sympathetic military officers and some decent Americans led to the return of the few survivors of internment in the humid regions of the South back to the Northwest's Colville Reservation. But Joseph was never allowed to return home to the Wallowa country, even though General Nelson A. Miles had promised to return Joseph and his people home. Joseph died on the Colville Reservation in northeastern Washington.

At the same time that the Americans were chasing Nez Perce refugees, they waged war on the buffalo, the wolf and the land. Buffalo hunters deliberately killed off the Great Plains herds, not really for their hides, but to kill the tribes dependent on the buffalo. In addition to human tribes, these included wolves and many other animals. The whites hated Indians and wolves the most. Hunters poisoned a bison carcass as bait—and killed wolves, coyotes, eagles and ravens. Jays, magpies, songbirds, wolverines, badgers, anything that would come to the kill also died. In 1915, following the demands of the public, federal policy demanded wolf extermination. This insanity lasted until the legislation of the Endangered Species Act.

A plan to bring Canadian wolves to the Yellowstone country and central Idaho was signed by then-Interior Secretary Bruce Babbitt in 1994. This plan called for state agencies to manage released wolves, but the states refused to cooperate. "The issue was too hot to handle," Wolf Recovery head Ed Bangs explained. "In Idaho, the Nez Perce said they would be happy to accept wolves."

Bangs said Nez Perce lands in central Idaho were a good
habitat for wolves: "They put together a good plan for wolf
management, so we contracted them for the program." Bangs
stressed that since Nez Perce were certainly Idaho "locals," not
outsiders like many pro-wolf supporters, they would understand Idaho ranchers' feelings. "Also, the Nez Perce revere
wolves—they have a different way of looking at animals,"
Bangs said.

Livestock growers were nervous about the planned wolf
releases, and they fought reintroduction. Despite their legal
arguments, the courts supported the return of the wolf. The
Nez Perce wolf-recovery plan combines scientific management
with traditional tribal concepts and beliefs. The tribe receives
$300,000 yearly in federal funds to support the wolves, and
works closely with the federal wildlife service.

Nez Perce call Wolf *He'me.* Wolf is an embodiment of past,
present and future to them. Currently, there are more than
260 wolves in Idaho. The Nez Perce offered wolves homes on
their reservation lands. They work with the Wolf Education
and Research Center, which was founded in 1990. The tribe
and the center opened a wolf-education center in 1997. It is
home to eleven captive-born wolves who have been socialized
with humans. They cannot live in the wild, because they view
humans as friends and their trust would be betrayed. Levi
Holt, a Nez Perce who worked with the wolves, maintains that
wolf recovery helps return the Nez Perce and all people to balance, dignity and the right way to live. "Restoring the wolf,
protecting the wolf, sharing our lives with the wolf gives us a
chance to have our culture reborn," Holt says. "We know that

successful recovery will lead to delisting of the wolf. We know that some ranchers fear wolves will hurt their livestock. We know that if states take over wolf management and wolves are delisted, some people will hunt wolves. But our tribe will not take part in hunting wolves. People will not be allowed to hunt them on Nez Perce lands. We will honor our ancient relationships. What affects them, affects us."

Holt says that when he remembers everything the wolves and his own tribe have endured together, he looks at the wolves and prays, "We mourned your death. We were saddened by your exile. We rejoice in your return."

Many people consider the return of the wolf, the buffalo, the eagle and other species as fulfillment of prophecy. At the darkest time of slaughter, in the nineteenth century, a number of Indian prophets arose. From the Great Basin country of Nevada, a Paiute shaman named Wovoka, "The Cutter," prayed to God for the renewal of the world and the survival of Indian people. God taught Wovoka a prayer dance. Wovoka called it "The Father's Dance." God told Wovoka that all people, Indian and non-Indian, must put aside their differences and live together in peace. All people were encouraged to dance the Father's Dance. Wovoka sent emissaries throughout the West and had many apostles, including white Mormons. Many tribes embraced the prayer.

The majority of Americans called this prayer the Ghost Dance, and they feared it. They feared what they did not understand. Federal response to the Father's Dance included the massacre at Wounded Knee and the outlawing of tribal reli-

gions. But the United States government did not understand
the point of Wovoka's prophecies and prayers. The Ghost
Dance was a prayer for the restoration and preservation of the
world and life. It was not a dance of death. It was a prayer for
restoration of the buffalo, the wolf, the game, the land, the
water, the people; all life. Today, many people feel that these
prayers have been answered, and that the return of the wolf is
one example of this fulfillment.

The hearts of the invaders have changed, shaped by the
land and its spirits. The land is home to all, and sacred to all.
Many finally understand this and struggle to restore and protect it. The growth of understanding and demand for change
have resulted in legislation like the Endangered Species Act
and the establishment of sanctuaries and wildlife refuges. For
those that equate life and Nature with beauty and the right
way to live, these are good things. It is ironic that the same
agencies that destroyed so much have bowed to public pres-
sure and now have restored so much. Prophecies are fulfilled
in strange and unexpected ways.

The Struggle Continues

The survival of wolf and world is far from assured. All of us,
all living things, are dancing on the razor's edge. Forces of overpopulation, poverty, ignorance, global markets and psychotic
capitalism challenge the survival of the natural world. Accumu-
lation of pollution and greenhouse gases due to global industri-
alization and the emergence of Hydrocarbon Man have literally

torn holes in the ozone layer—holes in the sky. Global warming is melting the polar ice caps and the tundra is receding. Every day, hundreds of species of plants, birds, mammals, reptiles and amphibians are destroyed due to land development.

Human fascination with machines and engines and the power of the oil industry threaten the small gains made in the last few years. More and more people buy cars and the gasoline needed to run internal-combustion engines. Madison Avenue creates markets and artificial needs, and consumers rush to fulfill these newly discovered needs. The world's people seek to imitate the glamorous consumptive lifestyles depicted in Hollywood films and on American television. The cycle goes on and on. Human beings know that they have a responsibility to share the world with one another and with other creatures, but most people are focused on the daily struggles for survival and do not think about how their actions affect other lives. All over the world, people see the results of neglect, abuse and devastation of the natural world, but still it continues. It is not simply a function of corporate greed—people demand the goods and services offered by the companies. People make decisions to buy cars and petrol; to build dams and destroy rivers; to punch into aquifers to slurry coal and to irrigate deserts. People decide to sacrifice wild regions to drill oil, to mine minerals, to build shopping malls.

The rain forests, a source of oxygen and water, continue to be burned because expanding human populations need land. Oceans are poisoned, used as dumping grounds for industrial waste. Irresponsible members of the mining industry use ar-

senic and other poisons in extraction and refinement procedures. Radiation leaks from nuclear submarines contaminate
water for coming generations.

The issue revolves around people accepting responsibility
for their actions. It is easy to complain about high petroleum
costs and the destructive aspects of an oil-driven world, and
then pay the price to run the automobile. But people can also
organize and stand up against destruction of life and accept
personal responsibility for their choices and actions. They can
choose to work with sustainable resources and products, and
to limit family size or not to have children. Corporations can
choose to operate as ecologically and personally responsible
entities and still make profits. Governments can put the best
interests of the future of seven generations ahead of corporate
and political cronyism. An epidemic of human irresponsibility
has swept the planet. People should study lessons from wolves
and learn about commitment and responsibility. But it is eas-
ier to complain and accept destruction as a sign of progress.

Politicians make promises to everyone. They face the pressures of megacorporations with money, power and stockhold-
ers concerned only with profit; as well as the demands of their
individual constituents. In democratic countries, a power
struggle between the rights of the community and oligarchic
commercial interests is emerging. Just a few years ago, officials
of the Nigerian government, following instructions from
Royal Dutch Shell executives, executed a Nigerian environmental activist because he stood up for Nigerian villagers. The
villagers demanded that the oil company develop ecologically

sound plans for oil extraction. They demanded development that would protect lands, animals, plants and people and would ensure that villagers share as partners in oil profits.

One of the clearest examples of the struggle between corporate oligarchy and popular will is the ongoing fight to preserve Alaska's Arctic National Wildlife Refuge. Located in northeastern Alaska and bordering Canadian territories, this refuge is America's northernmost sanctuary and one of its largest. It belongs to all Americans and is managed by the U.S. Fish and Wildlife Service. The wildlife refuge system was established to protect wildlife and habitat for American citizens now and in the future.

The refuge consists of almost 20 million acres of tundra, mountains, shore, lagoons, rolling hills and forest. It is home to caribou, musk oxen, wolverines, snow geese, wolves and tribes of subsistence hunters—Inupiat and Gwich'in people. It is home to more than one hundred sixty species of birds, thirty-six species of land mammals, nine marine mammal species and thirty-six species of fish.

The Beaufort Sea meets the shore of the refuge. Icebound for eight months of the year, its ice pack is home to the polar bear and the seal. In summer, whales navigate the waters. South of the coast lies the tundra. In springtime, the Porcupine caribou herd comes here. It is their calving ground. Foxes and musk oxen are permanent residents. The majestic Brooks Range rises above the tundra. Sure-footed Dall sheep tread the mountain slopes. South of the range, the land becomes spruce and scrublands of the ancient forest. Beaver, moose, mink,

snowshoe hares, voles, shrews, lemmings and many other creatures inhabit forests, marshes and rivers here. This is one of the
few remaining places in North America where Nature retains a
semblance of balance.

Oil companies have been interested in the region since their
rise to economic and political dominance in the early twentieth
century, when they learned about reported oil seepages along
the Arctic coast east of Point Barrow. In 1923, a 23-million-acre
Naval Petroleum Reserve was established in northwestern
Alaska to guarantee oil supplies for American national secur-
ity needs. From the Second World War through the 1950s, this
area was the focus of extensive federal oil and natural gas
exploration.

During the Eisenhower era in the 1950s, development in
Alaska generated concern among the American people and
government scientists, who worried that corporate development would destroy natural systems. In 1953, federal agents
released a report, *The Last Great Wilderness,* and stressed that
the northeast section of Alaska should be protected.

In 1968, the biggest oilfield in North America was located
on Alaska state land in the Prudhoe Bay area, very close to the
Arctic wildlife-refuge region. Within a few years, oil was discovered on the North Slope. To the detriment of the land and
its creatures, plants and systems, an 800-mile Trans-Alaska
Pipeline was built from Prudhoe Bay to Valdez in south-central
Alaska to feed oil to tanker ships, which then transported it to
American and global markets. Oil companies were eager to get
into the Arctic National Wildlife Refuge as well. Congress de-

bated the matter for years. In 1978, the House enacted legislation designating the area as Wilderness. The Senate required wildlife studies and petroleum studies and delayed decisions about oil drilling or Wilderness designation. In 1980, the House accepted the Senate bill and President Carter signed the bill establishing the Arctic National Wildlife Refuge. In the law, Congress specified that "the production of oil and gas from the . . . Refuge is prohibited and no leasing or other development leading to production of oil and gas . . . shall be undertaken until authorized by an act of Congress."

Since that time, oil companies have consistently pressured Congress to open the lands. The American people steadfastly demand that the region retain Wilderness designation and protection. The tribes inhabiting the land do not want oil development. They need the caribou.

In 1987, a report to Congress by the Department of the Interior stressed that oil development would damage both caribou and musk oxen. The report stressed that oil development would hurt wolves, polar bears, wolverines, snow geese, seabirds, shorebirds and fish. It pointed out that oil development would destroy subsistence lifestyles of tribes on both the American and Canadian sides of the border.

Public-relations spin doctors working for Big Oil refer to the wildlife refuge as "ANWR" when they meet with media or politicians. By using the acronym, they need not mention the words "national," "wildlife," or "refuge." Rather, they stress the national need for oil and the American "dependence" on "foreign oil," and they say that the land, the sea, the tundra

and the ice are "ugly." In Congress, it is a constant struggle
between lobbyists for Big Oil, Alaskan business interests and
environmentalists, the popular will and the needs of living
beings in the refuge. Congress took no action about the sanctuary after the 1989 Exxon Valdez oil spill. In 1991, a provision
to open the refuge to development was dropped from the National Energy Policy Act. But Big Oil keeps trying to destroy
it. In 1995, Congress supported budget legislation that included permission for drilling in the reserve. President Clinton
vetoed the bill, maintaining that life must be protected and
systems must be preserved in the refuge.

When Texas oilman George W. Bush and Dick Cheney, of
global oil giant Halliburton, took the White House in 2000,
they made no secret of their determination to open the reserve
to drilling. Environmental activists, letters from American
citizens and indigenous voices and elected representatives re-
sponsive to the will of the people have kept the reserve safe, at
least for a little while longer.

United States Geological Survey reports from 2000 indicate
that, under current oil market conditions, there is a 50 percent
chance of obtaining nine months of oil from this region to sup-
ply America's consumption of 19 million barrels of oil every
day. The destruction of thousands of animal lives, loss of the
Porcupine calving grounds and disruption of traditional hunting and gathering peoples' lives is a horrific price to pay for a
mere nine months of oil. But the debate continues in Congress,
despite determined American resistance to opening the reserve.

Meanwhile, thwarted in their attempts to destroy the

refuge, the Bushites and their oil cronies have turned their attention to the balance of the Alaskan Arctic region, as far west as the Chukchi Sea. They have jettisoned environmental safeguards on Alaska public lands and continue to threaten the land-use rights of Alaska's subsistence hunters. If they can't get into the protected refuge, they are determined to drill into and destroy everything around it.

The price of survival, democracy and freedom is vigilance: the land and lives of wolves, people and other creatures of northeastern Alaska depend on continued vigilance and on-going media and public education.

The world follows the American lead in many areas—culture, economics, politics, music and film. People closely watch American environmental policy. Many countries follow American conservation and preservation ideas. Environmental movements and organizations are growing across the planet. In places like Italy's Abruzzi region, small, shy wolves walk the oak and rosemary forests. In Romania, wolves live in forests and also on the edges of urban centers. In Mongolia, traditional herders respect wolves and worry about wolves bothering their livestock. But human demands often supersede ecological sense. Somehow, a workable compromise must be made. All of life lies in the balance.

With the fall of the Soviet system, many new governments emerged. In eastern Siberia, tribal peoples are struggling to reassume control of their own destinies. They face pressures from oil companies, the timber industry, trophy hunters and poachers. They face poverty, hunger and financial crises. They have not had much time to develop strategies to protect and manage their lands and wildlife. As a result, they are besieged by outsiders seeking to exploit these resources. They need economic stability and cold, hard cash. But they also want sustainable development and sustainable futures.

The onslaught of foreign developers, mining groups, oil companies and hunters is destroying those vestiges of natural systems that somehow survived Soviet exploitation. A recent dispatch from Aleksandr Semyonva, a Koryak man of Kamchatka, indicates that things are out of balance and wolves are extracting vengeance.

In his statement, translated by ethnologist Martha Madsen, an Alaskan married to a Russian and residing in Kamchatka, Mr. Semyonva expresses his distress at the changes his homeland is suffering.

> In an endless, bleak snowy blizzard stood a group of emaciated wolves, standing together on the tundra. In search of food, they migrate together . . . They've been looking long and hard for food . . . Suddenly, the leaders sensed the smell of meat . . . lots of meat . . . they break into a run, stopping briefly, noses working. Breathing in the tempting smell of meat, they rush toward the aroma of food, people, camp, and a herd of reindeer. As if by command, they halt and stand together in unison, then they break away running in toward the smells.

The man explained that the wolves divided into two groups, following instructions from the pack leader, closing in for the attack.

The reindeer also sensed the wolves and tighten up, running in a circle, threatening the edges with their antlers held toward their enemies. But the famished wolves aren't afraid of antlers or hooves. On signal from their leader . . . They raced directly into the center of the panic-filled reindeer, scattering them over the tundra. Now it will be easy for them to select and chase down their prey, one by one. The herders come running, but they may not get there in time.

The Koryak explained, "Now, already for fifteen to twenty years, wolves try more and more to harm people. [Even after eating his fill] the wolf runs for the herd and keeps killing reindeer . . . Wolves are some of the most intelligent . . . and sly predators on earth. With all of this, the wolf is also very vindictive."

Mr. Semyonva attributes strange changes in wolf behavior to modern human abuse of Siberia's lands and animals. "Contemporary tundra life is completely different than the old ways," he explained. "With today's vehicles, aviation and with the ease with which people began to kill wolves; the predators began to take revenge. People tried to destroy wolves, enraging them. Now they kill not from hunger or to hunt the herds, but just to harm people, to get revenge."

He continued, "For some time now, tundra dwellers don't follow the old traditions, habits, and ways of our ancestors. Already many forget. Few elders remain who are able to teach something. By legends and stories of my parents I know that

in the earliest times, wolves were much admired, and were
honored with their own celebrations and ceremonies. If wolves
began to harm people, it means the times have changed."

Mr. Semyonva explained the ways of wolves and how traditional Koryaks interacted with them. "The she-wolf was always
the head of the family," he said. "She trained and taught her
wolf pups to hunt and to stalk. They lived by how well she
taught, everything was done well and easily. If a hunter killed a
she-wolf, she wasn't immediately brought into the yurt . . . We
gather in joyful meeting of her. We . . . brought fire so that the
guest—the wolf, could lay a hank of her fur in the fire. (People
did this for her.) If the tuft of fur burned quickly, it meant
guests come with good intentions. People feel joy toward her.
(This tradition is preserved still so that if you go visiting or if
guests come to you, a handmade item of leather is . . . thrown
into the fire and people take from your clothes something—a
little piece of fur or wool and burn it in the fire.)"

The Koryak continued his recollection, "That is why they
wore hides with uncut-off heads. They brought the wolf into a
circle around the hearth . . . as the sun rotates; they laid it on
the east side of the fire with the head toward the fire. They
[put in front of] the eyes and ears some dry birch twigs, so the
[wolf] guest couldn't see how much reindeer and meat were in
the house."

Mr. Semyonva explained that his people offered the wolf-
spirit the "most delicious, fattest piece of meat. In this way,
people won over the wolf pack. They killed only white, fat
reindeer for the guest wolf. Wolves didn't harm us much. Our

people admired bears, wolves, reindeer, raven and eagles, fish. We lived off Nature and completely adored her. Now we have very few elders who still know of our past tundra life. This probably is our last generation that abides by . . . what we knew and did in our past."

This Koryak account of angry wolves coincides with other Siberian and Mongolian customs instructing people never to hunt and kill wolf cubs or to enter a wolf den to do harm. Tradition teaches that if people kill wolf cubs, their wolf families will come and hunt the transgressor. Siberians struggle to find a balance, like other indigenous peoples and those who seek to restore natural systems and learn to live within ecological limits. Perhaps the wisdom of the surviving elders can teach us how to make good use of available resources in post-industrial societies. Perhaps old knowledge can blend with techniques of scientific management and open new chapters in human and animal histories.

American wolf-recovery efforts clearly demonstrate that there is room enough in the world for both humans and other species. *Homo sapiens* is supposed to be the most sagacious of the animals. There is no need for people to destroy the planet and all of her beauty. The American people made deliberate decisions to restore endangered species and share the world with other creatures. Perhaps, with education and determination, people throughout the world can relearn ways of living in harmony with other beings. People must make hard decisions to live simply, to protect land and to incorporate respect for Nature directly into their daily business and personal lives.

Solutions are not easy, but through small steps, some recovery
has succeeded. Maybe someday, this recovery will encompass
the globe. Maybe there will be room and resources enough for
all life. It is a matter of choices and decisions. Responsible
choices insure survival and the ongoing dance of life. Lack of
vision and bad choices will destroy the natural world and lead
to oblivion. Navajos have a word which exemplifies striving for
harmony with all things; it is *hozho,* "Beauty." The Beauty
Way prays:

> With Beauty above me, may I walk
> With Beauty below me, may I walk
> With Beauty beside me, may I walk
> With Beauty all around me, may I walk
> May it be done in Beauty
> Walk in Beauty

May we all walk in Beauty.

Afterword

It seems like new information and research emerges about wolves every day. As I completed the *Wolfsong* manuscript, I received packages of information with updated wolf research from Italy, Finland, Kamchatka and Montana. Despite ancient relationships between humans and wolves, be they respectful or adversarial, the advent of genetic mapping, DNA analysis, radio collars, microchips and remote tracking has helped field researchers and revealed much new information. Expanding public interest in wolves and educational efforts to destroy old stereotypes contribute to more support for wolf and healthy ecosystem survival. It gives some hope for the future.

People who work so hard to bring creatures and ecosystems back from the brink of oblivion deserve respect and gratitude. Legislators who listen to their constituents, who introduce and support laws protecting endangered species, clear air and clean water and make sure there are land, money and personnel to support projects deserve thanks. Environmentalists, activists and organizations devote their lives to vigilance. Wildlife workers, whether government, private or volunteer, do this work not because it is lucrative, but because they believe in and love what they do. Nature centers, zoos, animal sanctuaries and rehabilitation programs all contribute. Too many suffer from budget cuts and financial challenges. These people give their time, their futures and sometimes even their lives for the creatures they love. They are rebuilding legacies that belong to everyone.

People must understand that wild creatures need wild lands. Certain places must not be developed. Animals, plants and people need space, clean air and clean water. Also, people cannot treat wild creatures and ecosystems like cartoon characters. They are beautiful and each has its own personality. Wolves rarely attack people, but people must respect wolves' territories and space. In Yellowstone, I have seen tourists walk up to buffalo and pull on their horns or have their children stand right beside the massive creatures for family photo sessions. Such animals are wild and unused to the strange ways of tourists. Many people do not know how to behave in wilderness. Predators are disinterested in eating people, but human ignorance and misbehavior can lead to tragic encounters and consequences. Respect and common sense are keys to living— Nature does not suffer fools.

Working with wildlife rehabilitation and living close to Nature in remote places like northern Arizona and Montana led me to write about the things I love. Living with and writing about wolves, ravens and crows enriches my life and gives me both sorrow and joy. It is a great privilege to care for wild creatures and help them heal when they are hurt. There is joy, relief, anticipation and fear when a bird or animal one has helped is returned to the wild. Like anxious parents, we hope for the best and fear for the worst. When we lose one, even though death is part of life, it still hurts.

I wrote *Wolfsong* to honor Mowgli, a wolf. He was born with a defective liver. We had almost two years together. Through *Wolfsong*, I wrote myself home again; to the mountains, mesas and forests of northern Arizona. I walked again with Mowgli and looked into his beautiful face and golden eyes. I breathed the pine-scented air of the San Francisco Peaks and heard *kachina* voices on the wind. Mowgli was the vehicle that led me to intensive study of the wolf: wolf nutrition, wolf behavior, wolf evolution, wolf myth. Mowgli and his family taught me many new things and revelations. Mowgli gave me a new appreciation of Aldo Leopold. He led me to read Lois Crisler. Mowgli led me to write about the reintroduction of Mexican wolves into the Mogollon country. He led me to Wolf Haven International and a deeper study of wolves and men. Mowgli led me to consider an appointment with a college in Montana and a return to Wolf Country. The greatest expression of thanks I can offer his memory is to teach others about his kind and work to teach others how to share the world. Mowgli was a wonderful wolf ambassador. He brought great beauty to the world.

The San Francisco Peaks are special mountains, sacred to the tribes of the Great Southwest. Hopis call them *Nu-va-tuqua-ovi*, Snow Village. They rise high above the Colorado Plateau to an elevation just over 12,000 feet. Hopis maintain that this is the perpetual home of the kachinas—earth, water and Nature spirits and the spirits of good, departed Hopis. The peaks are dotted with ancient shrines and indigenous herbal gardens. For many years, I worked with the tribes to defend the mountains from developmental destruction. I learned many things from the Hopi priests and Dineh medicine people. In working with wildlife rehabilitation now, I frequently remember one Hopi prayer in particular—one appropriate for the world today:

> Let there be life
> Let it be a long life
> Let it last forever

Annotated Bibliography
& Source List

A variety of sources, interviews, field notes, ethology reports, books and articles were used in research for *Wolfsong*. Much speculative work has been written about wolves, and they are the objects of folklore and propaganda. It was only in the twentieth century that wolf behaviors became the subject of serious field observation. My work uses an interdisciplinary approach to understand wolf and human interactions and the history that both have built together.

The people who knew wolves best were those who lived closely with them, the old Paleolithic hunters, shepherds who protected their flocks from predators, the tribes in both hemispheres who honored them. Ancient voices sing out in the old myths and legends. That is why *Wolfsong* opens with myth, to begin at the beginning. Many storytellers and knowledge-keepers shared old tales with me and gave me stories for my own—very special gifts. In many cultures, stories are personal property, much the same as family heirlooms or expensive regalia and jewels. To be gifted with such treasures and allowed to share them is more valuable than gold.

Despite tragic aspects and the near-destruction of wolves by people, the saga of wolf and human continues. Modern techniques and the determination of preservationists to restore wolves to parts of their ancient domain have opened a new era in understanding between Wolf and Man. With modern field techniques and enlightened attitudes based on observation and fact rather than fear and superstition, more people are learning to accept wolves as an essential part of a living, balanced world.

The stories my grandmother told me, my studies of world religions, shamanism, Graeco-Roman, Celtic, Finnish and Viking myths and my formal training in folklore and field observation provided the basis for this research. Caring for captive wolves and learning about federal efforts at wolf res-toration while working as a journalist provided deeper insights. Field observations of the Mexican wolf in the Gila country, where Aldo Leopold had his preservationist epiphany and learned to "think like a mountain," and observations of the Lamar Pack in the Yellowstone country further enhanced my knowledge. There is much more to learn about wolves and their roles in natural cycles, but the following source list serves as a good starting point for those who want to develop a foun-dation of wolf knowledge and wolf-lore.

Published Sources

Bakeless, John, ed. *The Journals of Lewis and Clark.* New York: Mentor Books, 1964. A concise, portable edition of the Corps of Discovers' field notes, with an insightful introduction by the editor.

Brandt, Anthony, ed. *The Journals of Lewis and Clark.* Washington, D.C.: National Geographic Society, 2002. A new edition with an Afterword by the Smithsonian's Herman Viola.

Crisler, Lois. *Arctic Wild.* New York: Lyons Press, 1999. Reprinted from the original 1956 Curtis Publishing Company edition. Crisler's work is a moving and powerful testimony to her love of Nature and wild things. Her adventures in raising orphaned wolf cubs while following migrating caribou on the tundra during her husband's filming of *White Wilderness* are remarkable. Her work revolutionized American attitudes toward wilderness and wolves. A foreword by wolf biologist L. David Mech, founder of Minnesota's International Wolf Center, points out that before 1956, only two books had been written about wolves: Adolph Murie's *The Wolves of Mount McKinley,* and Stanley P. Young and Edward A. Goldman's *The Wolves of North America.*
 Crisler was a beautiful, sensitive and compassionate woman. The world lost her in June 1971, but her love of wilderness and her light shines through her books, *Arctic Wild* and *Captive Wild,* and her many articles and columns. Through her writing, she remains a vigilant advocate for wolves and the living world.

Krueger, Sarah. "Red Wolf Report." June 2004. www.fieldtripearth.org. Updates on the recovery of America's littlest wolves, by the federal field director.

Lange, Karen. "Wolf to Woof." *National Geographic.* Washington, D.C., June 2002. An entertaining and interesting article about the evolution of wolf to dog and human-lupine-canine connections.

Lehman, N., P. Clarkson, L. D. Mech, T. J. Meier, and R. K. Wayne. "A Study of the Genetic Relationships Within and Among Wolf Packs Using DNA Fingerprinting and Mitochondrial DNA." *Behavior and Ecological Sociobiology*, 1992.

Leopold, Aldo. *A Sand County Almanac.* New York: Ballantine Books, 1966. An environmental classic, Leopold's experiences and love of the wild and his conversion from wolf killer and bounty hunter to preservationist and wilderness advocate are detailed in his essays. His chapter "Thinking Like a Mountain" documents his turning point and the beginning of his wilderness epiphany.

Lopez, Barry. *Of Wolves and Men.* New York: Scribners, 1978. One of Lopez's best works, a valuable resource leading to the work of other writers and naturalists as well as insight into wolves, ravens and people.

Luckert, Karl. *The Navajo Hunter Tradition.* Tucson: University of Arizona Press, 1986. An in-depth, interdisciplinary field study involving the most ancient aspects of old Dineh (Navajo) traditions, which links the heart of the House Made of Dawn directly with the heart of Siberia, through the vehicle of sweat lodge, hunting magic and archaic Athabascan language. It helps Navajo and non-Navajo understand Dineh ceremonialism and life-ways before the Holy People and the Spanish brought livestock to Navajoland. A masterpiece of work in the history of religion.

MacAllister, Mark. "Red Wolves of Alligator River." www.nczooedwolf. org. A history and study of the diminutive red wolf of the Southeastern United States.

Maud, Ralph. *A Guide to British Columbia Indian Myth and Legend.* Vancouver: Talonbooks, 1982. A well-written history of myth collecting in British Columbia and a survey of published texts.

Mech, L. David. "The ecology of the timber wolf (*Canis lupus lycaon*) in Isle Royale National Park." University, Agr. Ext. Sta., Ph.D. Thesis.

————."The Wolves of Isle Royale." Natl. Parks Fauna Ser. 7, U.S. Gov. Print. Office, 1966.

————. *The Wolf: The Ecology and Behavior of an Endangered Species.* New York: Natural History Press, 1970.

————."Wolf-pack buffer zones as prey reservoirs." *Science.* New York, 1977.

————. *The Wolves of Minnesota.* Stillwater, Minn.: Voyageur Press, 2000.

Mech with T. J. Meier and J. W. Burch. "Denali Park Wolf Studies: Implications for Yellowstone." *North American Wildlife and Natural Resources Conference*, 56:86-90, 1991.

Mech with J. M. Packard. "Possible Uses of Wolf (*Canis lupus*) Den Over Several Centuries." *Canadian Field Naturalist*, 1990.

Mech with P. C. Wolf and J. M. Packard. "Regurgitive Food Transfer Among Wild Wolves." *Canadian Journal of Zoology*, 1999.

Mech, L. David "Leadership in Wolf Packs." *Canadian Field-Naturalist*, 2000. What can one say about L. David Mech? He has devoted his life to the study and preservation of wolves, and works to educate the world about their true nature. We owe much to his hard work.

Murie, Adolph. *The Wolves of Mount McKinley.* Seattle: University of Washington Press, 1985. In 1935, National Park Service biologist Adolph Murie was assigned to investigate the decline of numbers in Mt. McKinley's Dall sheep herds. Murie studied the sheep from 1935 to 1942, and produced his report, "The Wolves of Mount McKinley." He concluded that disease and changing weather patterns were causing the decline, but he could not completely rule out the role of wolf predation in contributing to the decline. His field work was the first published research monograph about wolf ecology. He studied the Toklat wolves, and his experiences with them and in raising a cub he took from them forever influenced his perceptions of wolf life. The book was a best-seller.

Nelson, Edward William. *The Eskimo About the Bering Strait.* Washington, D.C.: Smithsonian Institution Press, 1983. Originally published in 1899, Nelson made extensive ethnographic and field observations among the Arctic peoples.

Nelson, R. K. *Make Prayers to the Raven: A Koyukon View of the Northern Forest.* Chicago: University of Chicago Press, 1983. In this beautifully written book, Nelson presents a sensitive portrayal of his life among the Koyukon people, and presents wolf and raven encounters.

Young, Stanley P., and Edward A. Goldman. *The Wolves of North America.* New York: Dover, 1944. A two volume compendium "covering the entire Christian era" and human-wolf relations. Essentially, a history of wolf destruction, but includes field reports, field notes, drawings and descriptions of wolf behaviors. Some information is inaccurate, much of the material is dated, but it is a valuable piece of historiography.

Zoroaster. *The Zend-Avesta, Pahlavi Texts.* www.sacred-texts.com/zor.

———. Avesta—Zoroastrian Archives. www.avesta.org/avesta.html.

Interviews with the Author

CHEYENNE

Conrad Fisher, Cheyenne Cultural Affairs, Chief Dull Knife College, Fall 2002–Spring 2004. Lame Deer, Montana.

Lawrence Whitedirt. Meetings with Catherine Feher-Elston, Fall 2002–Fall 2003. Lame Deer, Montana.

Alonzo Spang. Discussions with Catherine Feher-Elston, Chief Dull
Knife College, Fall 2002–Spring 2004. Lame Deer, Montana.

CHEYENNE-DINEH (NAVAJO)

Navajo Ranger Jon Dover, Cultural Resource Specialist, Western
Navajo Agency. Field work with Catherine Feher-Elston, Fall 1988–
Spring 2003. Tuba City, Dilkon, Giant's Chair, Flagstaff, Arizona.

COMANCHE

Stan "Bud" Morrison. The Valley Hi interviews with Catherine Feher.
Summer 1979–Winter 1980. San Antonio, Texas.

CROW

Rabbit Knows-Gun. Interviews with Catherine Feher-Elston, Winter
2003. Billings, Montana.

KORYAK OF KAMCHATKA, SIBERIA

Aleksandr Semyonva, translated by Martha Madsen of Kamchatka.
Winter 2003. Kamchatka, Russia.

KWAKIUTL

George Taylor, October 1990, Victoria, British Columbia.

LAKES BAND OF NORTH CENTRAL WASHINGTON

Kaye Hale, October 1990. Museum of Native American Cultures,
Spokane, Washington.

MICMAC

Russel Barsh, September 1990, Seattle, Washington.

NAVAJO

Miller Nez, medicine man, origin stories and travel prayers, prayers to
mountains, discussions and interviews, 1981–1983, Navajo Reservation
and Grand Canyon, Arizona.

Various traditional people from Big Mountain, White Cone, Chinle,
Teec Nos Pos and Coppermine, Arizona.

SNOHOMISH
Jack Kidder, September 1990, Snohomish Tribal Headquarters, Ana-cortes, Washington.

UNITED STATES FISH AND WILDLIFE SERVICE
Ed Bangs, Wolf Recovery Coordinator, Northern Rockies. Various interviews, February 2003–September 2004.

Tom Bauer, Mexican Wolf Recovery officer. News interviews 2000–2001 with Catherine Feher-Elston, Albuquerque, New Mexico.

David Parsons, Coordinator for Mexican Wolf Recovery, 1990. Flagstaff, Arizona, interviews, 1998.

WOLF HAVEN
Judy Loeven and Judy Palmquist, staff members with Wolf Haven of Tenino, Washington. Summer 2000, Tenino, Washington.

Index